Connecting Hearts One by One

Stories *of* Faith, Hope, Love *and* Unexpected Detours

M.A. Hammer

Foreword by

Jay Jacobs
Director of Athletics, Auburn University

Copyright © 2016 by M.A. Hammer

Connecting Hearts One by One
Stories of Faith, Hope, Love and Unexpected Detours
by M.A. Hammer

Printed in the United States of America.

Edited by Xulon Press.

ISBN 9781498486033

All rights reserved solely by the author. The author guarantees all contents are original and do not infringe upon the legal rights of any other person or work. No part of this book may be reproduced in any form without the permission of the author. The views expressed in this book are not necessarily those of the publisher.

Scripture quotations taken from the New American Standard Bible (NASB). Copyright © 1960, 1962, 1963, 1968, 1971, 1972, 1973, 1975, 1977, 1995 by The Lockman Foundation. Used by permission. All rights reserved.

Scripture quotations taken from the English Standard Version (ESV). Copyright © 2001 by Crossway, a publishing ministry of Good News Publishers. Used by permission. All rights reserved.

Scripture quotations taken from the New International Version (NIV). Copyright © 1973, 1978, 1984, 2011 by Biblica, Inc.™. Used by permission. All rights reserved.

Scripture quotations taken from the King James Version (KJV) – *public domain.*

www.xulonpress.com

Dear Gigi,

There are truly not enough words to thank you for introducing me to my newly aquired audience. The photo of you and Genny has put smiles on the faces of so many. I wish we had more time to visit... but please know you have touched my life and my heart in a very special and memorable way. God bless you sweet Gigi. When I think of my sweet Genny... I think of you. With love, Mary anne

Dedication

For my children, Elizabeth, Caroline, and Martin III, for your love and encouragement throughout this journey.
For my parents, K.K. and J.J., for your unconditional love and support and teaching me the importance of giving.
For my grandmothers, Ganny and Goggy, who encouraged me to write and showered me with love.
For Steve, there are truly not enough words for the encouragement and support you gave me throughout this journey.

Contents

Opening Remarks   Gigi Graham............................... ix
Foreword   Jay Jacobs, Director of Athletics, Auburn
                  University xi
Testimonials.. xvii
Introduction   My Book's Unlikely Detour xxi

1. Camp Hammer 33
2. Johnny's Lifelong Friend 39
3. G.G.'s Surprising Gift 43
4. A Blooming Relationship with Jan and M.E. 49
5. Learning from Annie 55
6. Behind Rosie's Smile 59
7. A Prescription from Dr. Swindoll 66
8. A Friendly Reminder from Darby and Ann 71
9. Dr. A's Permission Slip 79
10. The Tennessee Trucker 87
11. The Silent Angel 93
12. To India, With Love 98
13. Joshua and the Darkest Night 103
14. The Stranger 108

15. David's First State Dinner 113
16. Beverle's Boutique 119
17. Reggie's Grateful Heart 125
18. A Packed House for Muriel 130
19. Amy's Turn to Breathe 135
20. A New Chapter for John D 140
21. Oksana Searches for Answers 147
22. Deanna's Forty-Eight-Hour Plea 153
23. Bennett's Circle of Friends 161
24. Wheelchair Willy 166
25. Sophia and Grace: A Grandmother's Gift 171
26. Mary Queen of Our Hearts 179
27. Dez's Unforgettable Smile 186
28. Summer and Shawn 191
29. Celebrating Tina's Life 199
30. Ginger's Welcome Face 206
31. An Unlikely Group of Trojans 211

    Postscript 219
    Afterword 229
    Acknowledgments 237

Opening Remarks

Mary Ann's grandmother Ganny was an inspiration to me. Toward the end of her life, I'd sit and listen to her stories, which brought joy to my heart each time we'd visit. It's not so surprising that her namesake used "Aunt Mary's" legacy of faith, hope and love in her own stories. These delightful stories are written from the heart of a woman whose grandmother's example instilled a love for others along with the gift of storytelling. I'm honored to introduce you to Mary Ann, and the extraordinary group of people she holds close to her heart. May you be blessed.

Gigi Graham

My grandmother, Mary McKay Underhill,
and Dr. Billy and Ruth Graham's daughter, Gigi

FOREWORD

By Jay Jacobs, Director of Athletics, Auburn University

Mary Ann Hammer and her son, Martin, settled in to watch ESPN's College Football Game Day at home on a crisp autumn morning in 2015. She had only recently finished the book you now hold in your hands.

Just as you have no idea how profoundly *Connecting Hearts One by One* is about to change your life, I had no idea it was about to change mine. I had never even met Mary Ann Hammer. Then a touching TV segment neither of us will ever forget flickered to life in dazzling HD color on ESPN. That's where my connection with her begins.

It was a piece by ESPN's Tom Rinaldi, who even casual college football fans know is the best storyteller in the business. He has a gift for tugging at his viewers' heartstrings, just like Mary Ann does with her readers. Only she doesn't tug. She pulls and connects and plays your heart strings all at the same time, effortlessly making beautiful music like a perfectly tuned harp.

I'm the Director of Athletics at Auburn University in Alabama, and we were getting ready to play a big SEC game on that day Mary Ann and Martin were watching ESPN. I'll never forget what it felt like when Tom's piece on our team's "Unlikely Connection" with an inner-city school in Chicago came on with the nation watching.

Let me give you the quick backstory. It all started with an assignment at Schmid Elementary School on Chicago's Southside, where 90 percent of the students live at or below the poverty line.

Each grade selected a college for a video presentation on their chosen school's academics, athletics, and traditions. The second grade class picked Auburn University. When I first heard about the video made by these amazing young students, I initially thought it was just another interesting story. As the days passed and I watched their video, which would soon go viral, something told me I needed to learn more. I began to feel a force so strong that I got on a plane and flew to Chicago to meet these bright-eyed children.

We are in the business of making dreams come true, and as I watched the video again and again, even on the plane, I could see in their eyes and hear in their voices that these children had dreams, too. Somebody had to help make them come true. Why not Auburn University?

We landed in the Windy City and rolled through the Southside neighborhood toward the school. With two-sport legend Bo Jackson and our mascot Aubie the Tiger alongside us, I knew it was going to be a special day. As soon as I saw the children at the school, something that is hard to describe happened. I was forever changed by the look in their eyes. It burned deep in my soul. It quickly became an unforgettable spiritual experience. Because making dreams come true is what I believe in, the only thing I could think to do was find a way to bring those children to Auburn. I wanted them to see and feel the university they had worked so hard to learn about. I wanted to touch their hearts as they had mine. I had no idea what was to come.

Our visit electrified the small room of Chicago students and parents who heard what we were up to. We invited them to a football game and a weekend-long campus tour at Auburn, a thrill like Christmas morning for a group of children who had never flown on a plane or thought for one minute that college might be a possibility.

As I watched the ESPN piece, warm tears welled up in my eyes. Mary Ann was tearing up, too, and she was smiling.

She had been praying about who to ask to write the Foreword for *Connecting Hearts,* and she had a deep bench of heavy hitters with impressive writing credentials to consider. She'd even sent the manuscript to one noted Biblical scholar, but the package never made it to its destination. If it had, I might not have ever been asked to write this Foreword. When I look at the other names on this book's jacket, I have no doubt this was a divine encounter inspired by God.

That's the way He works, and I've come to learn it's the way Mary Ann works. She goes wherever the Lord leads her, even on unlikely detours that often lead to divine encounters with ordinary people who do extraordinary things. She listens to her heart and reaches out to the most unlikely people every day of her life.

As they were watching ESPN that morning, Mary Ann turned and asked Martin if he'd ever heard of me as my portion of the interview came on. Until I watched it again, I had forgotten I told ESPN "family and love has no boundaries" when they asked why we did it. Martin, a gentle soul who says few words but always seems to say profound things, looked a little startled by the thought of speaking with an Auburn Tiger. "Yes mom, I know who he is," he said. "But Mom. We're Gators." They are most definitely Florida Gators—with deep roots at the University of Florida and strong family ties throughout Florida.

Mary Ann then called my good friend Steve Dennis, who had been extraordinarily kind to Martin during his freshman year at Troy University, to see if he knew me. Steve laughed and told her we'd been close friends for years.

The amazing thing about this new unlikely connection? Mary Ann e-mailed and asked if I would read some sample chapters from the book and consider writing the Foreword. That may not sound so amazing until you know her e-mail explaining the book's title was *Connecting Hearts* came just hours before my wife and I were set to speak at an event for an adoption and foster parenting ministry in Montgomery. The name of the event? "Connecting Hearts." Many more Appointed Moments, as Mary Ann calls them, were made between me, members of my staff, and her in the days ahead.

The compelling stories in this book will do more than lift your spirits; they will ignite your faith no matter where you are in your walk. They will touch your heart and stir your soul. They might even change the way you live your life in a world that so desperately needs more of us to be humble and kind and helpful to those who need a little hope, just like those children in Chicago.

Imagine how different this world can be if we all realize something simple and profound. It's a lesson you will learn as you turn the pages: We're all connected. Rich or poor, black or white, or orange and blue—the colors the Gators and Tigers wear on football Saturdays in the fall—it doesn't really matter. Just like it doesn't matter if you're a Gator, a Buckeye, or a Bulldog, an NFL or an NBA fan. This book reminds us we are all on the same team: God's team.

I believe people love sports because sports are a lot like life. It's about the triumph of the human spirit. It's about overcoming adversity. It's about being connected to a team in pursuit of something greater than anyone can achieve alone. But there is a difference between sports and real life.

Foreword

As Mary Ann's stories remind us, life is not about competing against our fellow man. It's about connecting with them. It's not about winning or losing. It's about serving others and putting their needs above our own.

For me, life is as simple as the Great Commandments Jesus gave us: Love the Lord your God with all your heart, soul, and mind. Love your neighbor as yourself. Mary Ann does that every day.

I urge you to read one of these thirty-one remarkable stories every day for a month. I'm certain your heart will be forever changed.

Mary Ann shared with me that friends sometimes look at her, surprised by the unlikely things she does to help others, and ask a simple question: "Why bother?" Her answer is usually the same as ours when asked why we decided to fly to Chicago. "Why not? It's the right thing to do." Serving and loving unconditionally come with a cost. Helping others and being who God calls us to be come with a cost, yet loving our neighbors yields a return that can't be measured on a scoreboard, a balance sheet or the number of "likes" on social media.

Helping others is its own blessing. The return of being kind and selfless has eternal value that outlasts us all. Sometimes the adversity we face does make us ask the question: Why bother? Mary Ann Hammer's powerful book reminds us of the answer: *Why not?*

I'm blessed to have been asked to be a small part of this book because it reinforced one of my core beliefs. We can complain about the way things are, or we can do something about it. My hope and prayer is this book will touch your heart as deeply as it has mine. It has the power to help change the world.

Jay Jack

Testimonials

"Wow." If you've picked this up . . . pay for it and take it home. You won't want to put it down as God shows you what life is like when you let Him have your heart and in total trust, put your hand in His. Life takes on a deeper purpose and brings surprising joy as God connects your heart to the hearts of others in one divine encounter after another.

—Kay Arthur, president and founder of Precept Ministries, author and speaker

I have had the privilege of knowing Mary Ann and her family for many years. *Connecting Hearts One by One* is an amazing compilation of stories about the people that have shaped her journey and deepened her faith. Each story reveals the strength and inspiration that comes from connecting with others. It is through her relationships that she comes to better understand herself, her purpose and her gifts. Nothing short of inspirational.

—John Peyton, former mayor of Jacksonville, Florida, CEO and president of Gate Petroleum

Connecting Hearts One by One, is much more than one writer's memories or a collection of inspirational stories. Mary Ann has captured the importance of three of the most powerful words in history: 'Love Thy Neighbor.'

—Chancellor Jack Hawkins, PhD, Troy University

Eloquently written, *Connecting Hearts One by One* propels the reader through an assortment of emotions. It is the "heart story" of one woman's ability to find hope and guidance in the smallest and greatest of gestures that might otherwise go unnoticed. As we scurry through life, we are reminded to take notice, be less self-involved and more mindfully engaged with those around us. This book is an inspirational collection of my dear friend, Mary Ann's life tapestry, woven with but one thread, the gift of love for mankind.

—Jeri K. Millard, Founder and CEO of In the Pink, a non-profit organization helping care for women, men, children and families dealing with cancer.

CONNECTING HEARTS ONE BY ONE is one of the best written and most inspiring books I've read in a long time. It is a chronicle of life experiences and lessons learned through acts of kindness, love, and giving. Once you pick it up and begin reading these episodes in the life of Mary Ann Hammer, it is impossible to put it down. I know Mary Ann's parents, John and Kay Hammer, and they are some of the most loving and caring people I've ever met. Their home has a revolving door open to family, friends, and strangers alike, anyone who needs help or just enjoys kindness and hospitality. It is obvious that their faith, love, and hope in Jesus passed to Mary Ann. One message comes through loudly and clearly in this book. We should never be too busy to stop, look, and listen for opportunities to help, to show love, or give encouragement to those along our path. Those opportunities, as Mary Ann describes them, are truly DIVINE.

Art Williams,
Founder CEO of A.L. Williams Corporation, author

Testimonials

Great read! God is truly the wind in our sails as we journey through the sea of life. I am honored to know Mary Ann and her family and appreciate the impact they and her book have had on my life.

—Steve Dennis, former AD, Troy University, Director of Football Administration, Georgia Southern University

Mary Ann is a treasured friend and a beautifully gifted writer who bears witness to the power of the Holy Spirit at work in our everyday lives. The pages of *Connecting Hearts One by One,* are filled with captivating stories of faith, hope and love that leave the reader longing for the next one. You will be inspired and motivated into a deeper level of faith as you connect with the author and the individuals that she encounters in the divinely Appointed Moments. What an amazing testimony to God's grace and mercy amidst the storms of life.

—Vikki Cline, director of prayer at Ponte Vedra Presbyterian Church

Mary Ann has written from her heart a beautiful collection of stories that offer profound and inspiring insights into our relationship with God as mirrored in our relationships with each other. These vignettes are more like parables; they teach us, through example, how we can traverse our lives with faith, hope and love, by *"Connecting Hearts One by One."* I have known Mary Ann and her family for many years and have witnessed the many trials and tribulations she has endured courageously by the grace of her own faith, hope and love. Her stories beautifully illustrate that through our loving relationships we can all walk through life holding the hand of God.

—Gerard J. Budd M.D.

Introduction

My Book's Unlikely Detour

My book was nearing completion when I placed it aside for several months to have more time with my daughter, Elizabeth, during her emergency heart surgery. Then, on November 5, 2012, another unexpected occurrence happened—this time for me. An unsettling neurological event robbed me of my memory, of my daughter's heart ablation, my son's graduation from high school, his attendance at college, and, later, his interest in transferring to a school closer to home. In fact, everything—big and small—that had happened during the preceding two years was lost. For months, I had no recollection of that time whatsoever. As it turns out, a portion of my memory, even now, has been misplaced somewhere in my brain.

Of course I had questions. A lot of them, I might add. Learning I'd written this book, a dream I'd longed to accomplish from the time I was a teenager, was as much of a shock as the sudden memory loss itself. Even more shocking, this book I'd written was about thirty-one remarkable and inspirational people I'd known throughout my life. They were shopkeepers and handymen, an old man at the beach, a trucker from Tennessee, a humble chef—who had each shared with me a piece of their hearts and life lessons on helping others in the midst of adversity.

God was with me moment by moment; there was no doubt. I felt His presence whispering softly in my ears as His Word warmed my troubled heart. I was reminded He had ordered my steps since the day I was born and this day, and the unsettling ones that followed were no different. I knew in my heart that He was using these moments of uncertainty as a lesson in trusting Him. It was a lesson in giving Him the glory, regardless of my circumstances.

During the following weeks and months, I took a little side-trip, a "detour" of sorts, for medical treatment that included physical and cognitive therapy sessions. When I was stronger, I slowly began to retrace my steps. I opened my book, *Connecting Hearts One by One*, with excitement and trepidation. Although I knew the majority of the individuals in the stories, it felt like I was reading about them for the first time. As I turned the pages, I was reminded of Reggie's grateful heart and India's giving spirit and Rosie's gentle smile, and I was inspired by them once again. God placed a newfound joy within my heart as I reconnected with these special people. I became ever more determined to get well so that I could share their remarkable stories with people like you. First, I'd like to share some details of my life's unexpected detour.

On the morning of November 5, I awoke uncharacteristically late. My comfy down pillow seemed unusually hard and lumpy. I glanced at the clock. The bright-red LED digits read 8:45 A.M. Oh my goodness, I thought. Martin, my dependable and prompt high school senior, had overslept. I was used to his morning ritual of waking around 5:20, watching his favorite early morning TV show, eating breakfast, checking over his homework, making lists for the day, showering and then slipping into his familiar blue and white school uniform—all in that order, every day, for as long as I could recall.

Martin was dressed in khakis, a button-down shirt, and a golf sweater. *Why wasn't he wearing his school uniform?* I wondered. What was my particularly shy son doing in an unfamiliar and newly redecorated bedroom. "Martin," I said hesitantly, looking around a room that resembled a hotel room, not my cozy, feminine celery-green bedroom, "you're an hour late for school and you're not wearing your uniform."

At first my son smiled nervously, unsure of what I might say next. I felt his angst but had no idea what to do. For the first time in my son's life, the woman who was determined to "fix" life's little problems seemed to be having her own set of difficulties. As for me, I felt like a bleary-eyed bystander. I've had my share of dramatic moments, and as usual I convinced myself I could tip-toe through this worrisome incident without any problem! You might guess my typical response: *I'm just fine.* That was certainly an overstatement.

"Mom, go look out the window," Martin insisted.

I inched toward the draperies and pulled them back. It was a rainy day, the landscape alarmingly unfamiliar. "We're not at home are we?" I stammered. He shook his head uneasily.

I knew enough to try to keep things together for his sake. He's noticeably shy and soft-spoken. He definitely wasn't fond of change. In any other situation, I would have insisted on going to the ER. My thoughts felt distorted, confused, disorganized, and I wondered if I, a young fifty-year-old, could have experienced a stroke. Whatever "it" was, took me completely aback. I was aware enough to know I was either sick or somehow caught in a strange time warp. I was later reminded by my neurologist that my first order of business should have been taking care of myself—but quite frankly that's a whole other story as you'll soon come to find out.

We had only an hour to get ready for an admissions appointment at Newberry College. "Mom, we're in South Carolina, not Florida," Martin said. "Remember, I came to visit here a couple of months ago because I don't go to Troy University anymore?" Well, that was enough information to last me for quite some time. As I looked at Martin's slender frame and his doubtful eyes I wanted to tell him I would be just fine, so I did.

"I'll be okay, Coach," I said, an endearing name we call our favorite sports fanatic. "Things just seem a little foggy right now." He forced a smile. I sat quietly for a few minutes praying for God's protection and for Martin's interview.

"Mom, can we go now, are you doing okay?" Martin asked. I nodded. He walked closely beside me as we exited the hotel room and got into the car.

Somehow nearly two years of my life had vanished in an instant. Time, our time, had been misplaced. We were no longer preparing for his fall semester; fall semester had come and gone without a trace. Things looked and felt fuzzy. This only happens in movies or to people like my friend Annie or my grandmother, I thought, both of whom had succumbed to Alzheimer's years before.

At Newberry a friendly woman greeted us. "Welcome to our family," Ms. Atkinson said, gesturing for us to join her in a nearby conference room. I soon realized my usual keen sense of time and space was still not adding up. Cindy offered for me to wait in an administrative office while she interviewed Martin—an interview that seemed to last an eternity. When they returned, she asked me about his time at Troy University. I simply went blank. "What do you do Mary Ann," Cindy asked. Again, blank. At that moment something amazing happened. Instead of sitting back quietly with his head slightly bent as usual, Martin suddenly became my mouthpiece.

"She writes about God and people," he said confidently. I was absolutely blown away by the words of this beloved young man, a highly unassuming teenager, now assuming the role of my protector, without any obvious hesitation. In the absence of my ability to recall certain information, my quiet, socially awkward son fielded my vulnerability. He played the role of quarterback while I sat on the sidelines. It was a team effort I'll treasure for a lifetime.

At the end of the meeting, as we exited the admissions building, Martin began asking questions to jog my memory. "Do you remember when we went to play golf at my favorite course in South Carolina?" he asked. "Do you remember Mr. Dennis at Troy? Is your memory going to come back?"

I wanted to say yes to all his questions but he knew me too well. "You don't remember Mom, do you?" he said softly. By that time, I felt like I was standing in front of a trick mirror at the fair, and it wasn't funny or entertaining.

Throughout my life, I've found God tends to place me exactly where He wants me—and that is usually at His feet. On that cloudy, drizzly day, I was sitting right at His feet wondering, what next? I wanted answers, so did my family. Once we returned home—with Martin's adept driving skills—I scheduled an appointment to see my neurologist the following morning. He suggested I might have experienced a mild stroke. He gently explained I'd have to undergo a battery of tests, along with an intensive cognitive exam by a neuropsychologist to determine the severity of my memory loss, and if those memories might ever return. I was told that after several weeks of wearisome tests, the doctor would render his diagnosis.

The bottom line, after weeks of testing, my ability to process information had been compromised by a non-specific neurological event that had occurred at some point in my life. The physicians were unable to pinpoint an exact date. Cognitive therapy would be the first line of treatment. The final, and most distressing, diagnosis from the vast battery of tests I underwent led the team of doctors to strongly suggest I'd been suffering from a sometimes debilitating disorder called PTSD.

PTSD or Post Traumatic Stress Disorder hinders a person's ability to bounce back to a regular and healthy routine after a traumatizing event or set of events. For me, the very private and personal trauma I'd lived with over many years caused my brain suddenly without warning to shut down. My capable and trusted PTSD therapist suggested, "Much like a computer, unable to function without the proper power source, your brain determined that its power source had been drained to the point of "Power-Down Mode." I'd been running away from my pain and heartache for so long I lost sight of myself and my "power supply." The time had come to face the reality of those traumatic events. Events that caused me to lose sight of who I was and who had ordered my steps.

The days following my return home left my emotions surging like a tidal wave engulfing even the most routine affairs of everyday life. Phone numbers would light up on my "new" smart phone that I was unable to remember. My bank had changed its name and phone number, which I had previously committed to memory. My hairdresser Oksana was no longer my hairdresser—she had moved to another city to join her estranged husband, an answer to her prayers and mine.

Besides my daughter's emergency heart surgery, the most alarming event of all, my dearly beloved father had been diagnosed with cancer and was awaiting sixty treatments of radiation. These events in and of themselves are for the most part natural progressions in life. However, trying to process such heart-wrenching incidents in the span of one week left my head reeling.

Then I began to experience a mixture of unsettling occurrences mixed with flickers of sheer delight. I began to wonder with a sense of anticipation: Who will I run into today? Will some of my memory return? What are my family and friends thinking? Will my kids adjust to my lack of memory? Not until weeks later was I able to come to terms with these unexpected occurrences or "detours" that I began to refer to as "Appointed Moments." They were pre-arranged connections from the heart of Jesus to mine. They were moments God had placed in my life to remind me of a divine script He had created the first day my parents held me in their arms, on the same day I took my first breath outside the safe place of my mother's womb.

These Appointed Moments, I came to realize, were a part of God's sovereign plan. Not always what I expected, of course, but nevertheless His plan was in motion. His plan did not always include unspeakable joy or intense pain and sorrow. It was a mixture of both, and everything in between, appointed by The Master, for His child—just like the plan He has for you. A plan that is, at times, mysterious and even incomprehensible, but it is a plan from Jesus to you. A plan that might even seem unfair but, nevertheless, it's meant for good in the end. It's a promise from Jesus that says He knows exactly what each of us can handle, He knows we are all unique and for that reason He will never give us more than we can bear.

One morning I recalled a passage in the Bible from the book of Isaiah 55:8–13, "'For my thoughts are not your thoughts, neither are your ways my ways,' declares the Lord . . . 'So shall my word be which goes forth from My mouth; It shall not return to Me empty without accomplishing what I desire, and without succeeding in the matter for which I sent it.'" Though losing a considerable portion of my memory seemed unimaginable at the time, I was still led back to the Lord and the cherished group of people

He placed around me to enrich my life every day. He was teaching me to trust Him regardless of my circumstances—and it worked.

God has perfect timing. Remember it's all in His hands, I reminded myself. Over the next several months I started thanking God for these Appointed Moments, for all the unexpected detours and the amazing connections he'd placed in my life. I decided to look for the silver lining during this bewildering period. The good news: I could remember my early life and everything that had happened since November 2012. My doctors said I was making good progress. I "graduated" from cognitive therapy thanks to an angel named Ashley. She taught me ways to strengthen my memory skills and put me on a rigorous online program with various websites to increase my brain function. It was mind-bending, but absolutely worth the time and effort.

I then began the challenging task of meeting with a PTSD therapist who taught me how to breathe again, how to channel the disruptive parts of my life into a more positive way of dealing with my past. She reminded me that God is in complete control and all I have to do is listen to His voice. She too had dealt with similar traumatic events in her life, and therefore really understood my feelings. Again, God provided the right connection at exactly the right time I needed His help, and hers.

During this time, I learned that life rarely goes as planned. We must learn to adapt to the changes and the hurts in our lives. If we are blessed to have the Creator of the Universe steering our wheel, we are one step ahead of the chaos that sometimes leaves our hearts and bodies reeling out of control. There are times in our lives we ask why a job didn't work out, why an illness persists, why a loved one walked away. The answer: It's all part of God's master plan. Every disappointment, every delay, every difficulty isn't there to set us back—quite the contrary, these glitches are to set us up for God's blessings, for His Appointed Moments, for His healing.

He is the great physician. He is the all-knowing, all-loving God and His grace and mercy will prevail. All we have to do is wait patiently on Him, trust and obey and His blessings will overflow. By allowing Him to steer our thoughts and our decisions down an often rocky road, He always gets us to the right destination in spite of ourselves and our circumstances.

Much to my surprise, my oldest daughter, Elizabeth had been keeping in touch with my book editor, Elinor Griffith, once an editor at Reader's Digest, giving her progress reports on my health issues. One afternoon my phone rang and Elizabeth was standing by to receive the call. "Mom, it's your editor, Elinor." My editor, I thought, what will I possibly say to someone who's been such an integral part of my life and I can't retrieve the memories? Even more curious, what will she say to me? When I finally gathered my thoughts and composed myself, my daughter handed me the phone.

"Hello," I said haltingly.

"Well, hello, Mary Ann, how are you?" Elinor asked in a tender voice. She summed up our first meeting in New York—how we'd immediately connected. I had no doubt. Her encouraging words, her thoughtful questions and her familiarity with my book gave me a dose of hopefulness. Our subsequent conversations persuaded me to take a peek through the pages we'd shared for over a year; pages that led us to a mutual kinship. With Elinor's friendly nudges, I started to retrace my steps. Again, reading these stories, I started to reconnect with this group of people who changed my heart, one by one. All did so in so many different ways and all planned quite neatly by my Father in Heaven.

I rediscovered in this collection of thirty-one stories—a month's worth as it turns out—that I had sprinkled some of my favorite seedlings (quotes and verses) for you to reflect on. The wisdom in these words, some from everyday people, others from poets and saints, has helped to light my path as I trek through life's unexpected detours, and now hopefully will encourage you too.

At the end of the book you'll find "31+1 Simple Acts to Follow," again one a day for a month. Using this list as a guide, your efforts can also bring you closer to faith, hope and love. Your own "Vine of Simple Acts," as I call it, can flourish and help transform the hearts of one person... or maybe, even the world.

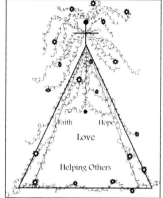

I realized any recovery process can be draining regardless of the illness. In those times of stress and frailty, that's where God extends His unfailing mercy, sending the greatest blessings of all. The truth is the book was a wonderful surprise for me. It wasn't just the book I had dreamed of writing since I was a teenager—it was so much more. The people and their stories lifted my spirits and renewed my faith—instilling God's unfathomable grace, once again.

Before my memory lapse, I'd never taken the time to grieve for past hurts, hurts that had left me feeling completely broken. I'd offered forgiveness, but I hadn't forgiven myself. God not only asks us to forgive everyone who has ever hurt us, He insists on it. That included forgiving me.

I hadn't paused long enough to realize God was walking beside me every step of the way. He was carrying me so that I might, in turn, carry others. The stories convinced me I was on a path where God was leading me moment by moment. His guiding hand took my hand, reminding me of the awesome blessings He continues to bestow upon my life. He is true to His word; He promises He has given us everything we need for life and Godliness. If God is for us who can be against us? No one! He promises

He won't allow anything to happen to us unless His hand is upon it to bring good in the end.

Although I'd lost significant memories, things really hadn't changed that much. My renewed faith, my hope for the future, and my love for other people were still intact. All of these detours of life, these unexpected moments of sheer delight and times of grief and sorrow had led me to write *Connecting Hearts One by One,* a book about people who I believe are a lot like you and me. People who want and need to connect to the hearts of others, just as Jesus did in His quiet, unassuming way. He knit His heart to the hearts of people who once were blind and broken and enabled them to see and heal in the name of FAITH, HOPE and LOVE. He made a connection with others that will forever bind those who know Him to His eternal home.

> "'I know the plans I have for you,' declares the Lord. 'Plans to prosper you and not to harm you. Plans to give you hope and a future.'"
>
> —Jeremiah 29:11

"But as for me and my house we shall serve the Lord."

—Joshua 24:15

1

Camp Hammer

"And now these three remain: faith, hope,
and love but the greatest of these is love."
1 Corinthians 13:13

When I was growing up my family was seen as prominent and socially connected, but my parents always insisted, "To those who have been given much, much is expected." We were taught to be eternally grateful for what we had and, as I would later find out, this charmed life we led could disappear in the blink of an eye.

As a young teenager, I was not overly impressed that my parents used their graciously appointed Colonial-style home in Tampa, Florida, to promote goodwill. How could they possibly have had time to entertain the homeless, pregnant teens, preachers and public figures in "our" house? What about us, I thought. What about our problems? The answer: we were far better off than we ever imagined.

The purpose of my parent's hospitality was clear. We should value people for who they are, not for what they have. Surrounded by a diverse group of individuals at our over-sized kitchen table, we learned the secrets to a fulfilling life: faith, hope, love and "doing unto others as you would have them do unto you."

The fine people who maintained our home were well-aware of our family's charge to help others in good times and bad. Oscar, the gardener, always tipped his hat and welcomed visitors to our home, "God bless ya'll," he would say. Robbie, our devoted housekeeper who was like our second mother, and Catherine, a fabulous southern-style cook, instilled their own prescriptions for life with a sense of humility and grace.

I well remember Robbie saying, "There will be no talkin' about other people in this house. No bein' a big ole snob, no, no. This is my house too. I'm here every day and I expect you children to act like ladies and gentlemen just in case one day you live in the President's house and have to think about a whole bunch of people who might need your help."

Robbie, of course, was referring to 1600 Pennsylvania Avenue, an address we had been privileged to visit for Christmas parties, but we had no interest in moving there! We already lived in a big white house, and that was more than enough for us.

My father referred to our not-so-modest home as "Camp Hammer." Sometimes he didn't know who all the campers were going to be, but he knew they would show up. Whether a group of teenagers coming over on Monday nights for Young Life Bible Study or a young unmarried woman who lost her baby before term and had nowhere else to go, Camp Hammer stood ready to welcome its guests. One time my younger sister, then a freshman at Wheaton College in Illinois, asked if she could bring a few friends home for spring break. Not until seventeen college coeds showed up did my parents realize this group might overwhelm the foundation of our guesthouse. Mother merely smiled, while dad scratched his head in disbelief.

The coeds learned to make my grandmother's famous pancakes, helped with odd jobs and spent hours in the pool. One afternoon, though, Dad packed all of them into a rented van to meet some homeless people living under a bridge who he visited on a regular basis. My father wanted to share with my sister's friends his desire to help others, while also showing them around town. On the last night at dinner, he asked everyone to join hands. My father thanked God for his "new friends," the good food, and then, with a grin, asked God to make these young people "fishers of men." He looked around at the coeds and quipped, "I'm no preacher kids, but I assume you know I'm not talking about catching the right guy." This grounded group of believers, all northern born, other than my sister, probably thought, *So this is what dinner in the south is like.*

Another time Joni Eareckson, founder of Joni and Friends, visited with us. A life-altering diving accident had left her paralyzed, feeling virtually helpless, but not hopeless. She'd learned to paint masterpieces with a brush between her teeth and had authored several books, along with a daily devotional, *365 Days of Hope*. In the midst of unimaginable adversity Joni's example of faith and genuine kindness amazed and humbled my family and me. Watching her create a beautiful painting of a flower before our eyes was a testimony to God's saving grace.

For my family, helping others was not an option. It was a way of life. Admittedly, it was not always first on my priority list. I always had a heart for others, but others included me! Things changed when I was seventeen. Biblical scholar Kay Arthur and her husband Jack, also esteemed guests at our home, hosted a summer boot camp that I attended near the mountains of Chattanooga, Tennessee. It wasn't an actual boot camp in the sense of physical endurance; it was an outreach program that helped curious teens learn more about God. This was a connection that took me some getting used to. At the time, quite honestly, I wanted to be on the tennis court back home practicing for my next big match.

One evening being quite homesick, I tried running away from boot camp in my mother's wood-paneled station wagon that I'd driven to camp. It is certainly something I'm not proud of, but it was an experience that led me to the beginning of my journey with the Lord of my life—a journey that didn't simply happen overnight. In fact, it took Kay Arthur herself tracking me down and leading me back to boot camp. After thirty-something years, we can now laugh about this story, knowing this too was an inspired connection, and an "Appointed Moment" that ultimately changed my life. By the way, having Kay Arthur strongly suggest I get my "little self" back to boot camp immediately was probably one of the most humbling experiences of my life, and thankfully life-changing.

On the night after being "captured" (actually rescued) by the greatest Bible scholar I know, Kay started the evening with a story that did transform my life and the way I viewed and treated other people. "My beloved," she began. Her eyes lit up as she shared the account of a plane trip she took and a conversation with the man seated next to her.

"Excuse me, ma'am," he said. "May I ask what you do?"

In her convincing and persuasive tone Kay stated, "I am an ambassador."

"For what country?" the surprised man asked.

"I am an ambassador for the Kingdom of Heaven, and I represent the King of Kings and the Lord of Lords."

What could anyone possibly say to that? Her compelling words I shall never forget. In considering Kay's bold statement of serving God as His ambassador, I began slowly to reach out to others. The thought of being an ambassador, without having to go through all the red tape of attaining such an honor, appealed to me. I had the chance to spread goodwill and didn't have to attend state dinners!

I left boot camp with a new appreciation for my family, my friends and the shielded world I grew up in. I still made mistakes and acted like a teenager, but I had a renewed sense of my family's charge: to those who have been given much, much is expected. Thanks to Kay, an unexpected detour back to boot camp allowed me to see Jesus instead of me.

Looking back on my life at Camp Hammer, there are a few things I would have changed, but not many. I'd learned that love covers a multitude of sins, life isn't always easy, forgive and be forgiven, live in abundant faith, embrace hope, and help others, again and again!

> ### A life lesson in... faith, hope and love.
>
> Childhood memories are different for all of us. I happened to be blessed to have a loving and supportive set of parents who came to know the Lord just in the nick of time. Our seemingly "perfect" family was falling apart at one point. My parents were close to divorce. And not until one of my siblings endured a life threatening accident and a five-hour surgery that could have left her paralyzed, did my mother learn an important lesson--she could not handle life on her own. She hid herself in a bathroom stall in the children's hospital asking Jesus to come into her heart and save her precious child, my sister. That prayer changed the life of my mother and eventually the rest of our family. At her weakest moment the Lord heard her prayer. She promised Him she would go anywhere and do anything if He would save her child's life. She stepped off of her social merry-go-round and fled to the arms of Jesus and she's still there today calling out His name and leading the broken-hearted into a life filled with hope and an abundance of grace. Camp Hammer is still alive and well while faith, hope and love guide us through unexpected detours, disappointments and a heap of divinely imparted, "Appointed Moments."
>
> *Thank You dear Lord for family. Thank You for the blessings of godly parents. Help us to be imitators of Christ, giving our children the tools needed for a future filled with faith, hope and love.*
>
> *Amen*

"Above all, love each other deeply, because love covers a multitude of sins."
—I Peter 4:8

"Blessed is the influence of one true, loving soul on another."
—George Eliot

"Of all the things Christ wants for us, loving Him and focusing our attention on Him, are the most important."
—Charles Stanley, pastor

2

Johnny's Lifelong Friend

"In all things I have shown that by working hard in this way we must help the weak and remember the words of the Lord Jesus, how He himself said, 'It is more blessed to give than to receive.'"
Acts 20:35

At seventeen as a high school senior, my father, John Hammer Jr., didn't have the highest grade point average in his class, nor did he wear a letter jacket. He felt most comfortable around the crowd of kids who had far less than he did socially and financially. He was seen as a popular leader, someone the students could go to for encouragement, support and a kind word or deed.

Not only that, but enough students considered him so admirable they elected him president of his school. He certainly appreciated the honor, but probably would have been happier out of the spotlight at the family farm, hunting, boating or fishing with his buddies.

At the end of the school year, Johnny was presiding over graduation ceremonies. As each student's name was called, he or she walked up the stage steps to receive a diploma. When the principal called out the name

Ben Pickney, there was silence. Johnny knew that Ben, whose muscles were nearly paralyzed with cerebral palsy, would have trouble climbing the steps to the stage. The disease affected his speech, his movements, his balance and his entire way of life.

It was important to help him with as little drama as possible. Johnny just did what he knew he had to do, for Ben's sake. Johnny already had this strong sense of compassion as a high school student, often a self-centered time. He felt a deep connection with people.

Without hesitation my father walked down the stairs, grabbed his friend's right arm and guided him to the middle of the stage and there, finally, Ben received his long-awaited diploma. A broad smile alighted on his droopy and wilted face.

The story, which I've heard recounted many times, doesn't stop there. Ben and my father stayed friends. After graduating from college, Johnny married his sweetheart Kay, and they eventually had four children, including me. As a teenager, I vividly remember Dad, by then a well-established insurance executive, taking us to visit a local market where Ben hung out. The look of surprise on Ben's face as we walked through the doorway touched our hearts.

Every Christmas morning growing up, for as long as I can remember, the phone would ring as we were opening gifts. On the other end of the line a garbled voice would ask to speak with "Johnny."

"Dad, the phone is for you," we would say in anticipation. "It's Ben calling."

My three siblings and I would drop our gifts and dash into the kitchen knowing Ben's call was our father's most-treasured gift. We would gather around the phone as they talked. At the end of each call, Dad's eyes would tear up and he would say to Ben, "God bless you and Merry Christmas, buddy."

In a muddled voice came, "Merry Christmas, Johnny, God bless you, too."

Today Dad's commitment to helping others—daily, weekly, monthly, yearly—remains unfaltering, a true inspiration for people around him. It's a journey, I might add, that continues to surprise even him.

One brisk morning, many years later, Dad was headed to meet his friend Don at a local coffee house near their mountain-top home, Camp Hammer II. Apparently, Don was running quite late, and my father started to worry. After making several attempts to phone with no answer, he proceeded cautiously around the narrow mountain roads in North Carolina leading to Don's farmhouse. As he approached the front porch, a man's voice was calling for help.

"I'm on my way, Don," yelled my father. "Hold on."

His friend had collapsed and was sprawled on his back. A puddle of blood swept the floor beneath him. My father pulled Don carefully across the hardwood floor, down the back steps into his nearby SUV and raced a few miles to the Highlands-Cashiers Hospital.

Upon seeing the nearly unconscious patient, the ER physician decided to life-flight Don to the nearest trauma hospital in Asheville, North Carolina normally an-hour-and-a-half drive away. Don was bleeding to death internally from a colon obstruction and required immediate surgery.

Thankfully the operation went well, and Don was able to go home a few days later. My father explained he had never helped before in such a dire medical emergency. "I never knew I was capable of saving a life," he said in disbelief.

Such life-saving action is, of course, unusual. Whether it's Don, Ben, or helping a crowd of others, my father's thoughtful and unassuming actions prove we can all make much more of a difference than we realize. When love abounds and God is at the helm, anything, absolutely anything, can happen.

A life lesson in... a servant's heart

My father was and is the greatest example of living every day of his life with a servant's heart. Whether helping his friend Ben, Don, or meeting new friends while receiving sixty rounds of radiation for his adenocarcinoma, he'd say, "I'm blessed to have so many people around me to support me and give me hope and love." He hurt for those who had no family, sitting with them as they awaited their treatments. One day in the waiting room, after receiving his treatment, he said to me, "Mary, I met another new friend, and my case is nothing compared to his." He'd pray for them each day, just as he did for his dear friends Ben and Don. As he awaits his fourth bout with yet another cancer diagnosis he says, "I know where I'm going, so let it be." I pray to be that trusting and positive every day. All it takes is faith in the One who is the giver and taker of life.

Dear Lord, allow us to have a servant's heart even on the days we can't imagine doing so. Help us to embrace Your saving grace and leave the rest at Your feet. Thank you, Lord, for holding us in the palm of Your hand.

Amen

"God has not called us to see through each other, but to see each other through."

—author unknown

"We make a living by what we get, but we make a life by what we give."

Winston Churchill, prime minister, British statesman

"I am Thy servant to do Thy will, and that will is sweeter to me than position or riches or fame, and I choose it above all things on Earth or in Heaven."

—A.W. Tozer, minister, author

3

G.G.'s Surprising Gift

"One, who gives freely, yet grows all the richer; another withholds what he should give, and only suffers want. Whoever brings blessing will be enriched, and the one who waters will himself be watered."

Proverbs 11: 24–25

John Milton Hammer Sr., or G.G., as we called my grandfather, gave in excess to those who had far less than he did. Once on a plane trip, for instance, he sat next to a young man who had just graduated from college and wanted to start a business of his own. G.G. reached into his back pocket and pulled out his wallet, lined neatly with cash and lots of it. He handed the surprised young man a $500 bill . . . that is when $500 bills were still around. Evidently, G.G. enjoyed carrying President McKinley around in his back pocket. The starry-eyed entrepreneur-in-waiting said, "How can I ever repay you." My grandfather replied, "Boy, just work like there's no tomorrow. That will be my repayment."

Sometimes that spirit of giving didn't extend to his immediate family. My father and my grandfather, both successful insurance executives in

South Florida, had a similar work ethic: work hard, work long, and put the client first, always. Yet somewhere between these two highly driven personalities, my grandfather's over-zealous competitiveness led to an unhealthy sense of control at times. He expected perfection, and sometimes he pushed the limits of that point of view.

As the oldest of four children in our loving yet firm household, I felt responsible for the family's well-being—not that I had the wisdom or the financial stability at age sixteen to do so! Still, I adopted the notion that fixing an individual's problems happened to be my specialty, especially familial ones. I thought if G.G. enjoyed helping others so much he certainly would want to do the same for his family.

When my grandfather objected to the differences between him and my father, I reminded him of the countless instances when my father had made a positive difference. A fair disciplinarian and an active director of family activities at Camp Hammer, Dad managed our home activities somewhere between "The Brady Bunch" and the latest TV reality show.

Being fairly naïve, I tried to subtly encourage G.G. to be kind to all people, especially his family. A couple days during the week I would stop by the business after school to check on the "climate" in the office. One afternoon, tip-toeing through the back door like many days before, I slowly pushed opened my grandfather's heavy wooden office door. I slipped in and put my hands over his eyes, whispering "Guess who?"

"Who's there?" he said in his deep southern drawl.

"It's me, G.G."

He placed his phone on speaker and motioned with his strong, weathered hands to come closer. "Come on over here, kitten," he said with authority.

When my grandfather called me "kitten" it often meant a positive change in behavior was looming in the atmosphere. While still talking on the phone, he swiveled his chair around to face me. Immediately he began to fumble with his left hand to extract his familiar leather wallet from his back pocket. As a teenager I was always amazed at the amount of cash he would scrunch into his soft leather cash depository!

"Ross," he said to the president of the local Coca-Cola bottling plant, "let me call you back. My oldest granddaughter is here to straighten me out, I think." Then he hollered to his assistant, "Hold all of my calls for a few minutes. Mary Ann is here visiting."

Actually "visiting" was simply his nice way of saying I think I might be in trouble.

I pleaded softly as I had done many times before. "G.G. can you please be a little nicer to dad? He loves you. Promise you'll try a little harder."

"Now kitten, don't you have anything better to do than to come by here and discipline your old granddad?"

I shook my head and said, "No sir."

At this point, my grandfather stood up and continued twisting and turning his wallet until it popped out. "Here kitten, now you get on home. I love ya'll." I gave him a kiss on the cheek and folded up the all too familiar twenty or fifty-dollar bill and placed it in my change purse.

"Now don't spend that all in one place. You hear?" Sometimes I would hand him a small notecard, similar to the Heartnotes I send to people now—*G.G., I love you and so does Jesus.*

Moments such as these became a common occurrence, and I wasn't going to stop trying. I giggled under my breath knowing G.G. might not be too happy with how I was using his latest "donation."

Instead of using the money for unnecessary things, I decided to save the secret payoffs for a preacher I had overheard my parents talking about at dinner one evening. The pastor had recently moved into town to raise money to build a new church. I wanted to be part of giving to someone who was spending his life "doing unto others" for Jesus' sake.

It seems ironic in retrospect that my first real random act of kindness was introduced to me by my grandfather, in a rather round-about way!

Although the payoff system he used to compensate for his sometimes insensitive treatment of my father was an unconventional way of my acquiring money as a teenager, it helped lead me on a journey in giving for the sake of others. So, without knowing it, my grandfather planted a seed of generosity in my heart. A clear choice then faced me. Instead of feeling defenseless, a badge of courage surrounded my young life with a sense of hope for the future, and his payouts became a surprising gift to help this humble preacher. I couldn't have enjoyed using the money for my own desires—that to me would have encouraged my grandfather's efforts to buy me off in a sense.

In my grandfather's later years, he too learned that giving was better than receiving, not only to others, but also to his family. When the time came for him to be with the Lord, he said, "Watch out for your family kitten, I'm ready to go home now." That bittersweet moment reminds me of a few stories my father told me later in life about my grandfather's generosity. My father had a friend named Tommy whose dad died at a very young age. G.G. was a close friend of Tommy's dad. Over the years, my grandfather included the young man in various trips and outings, and supported his fixing up old cars to sell for extra cash. Tommy became an adopted part of the family, giving him a close friend (my father) and someone (my grandfather) to stand in for his own his father.

G.G. was an avid golfer. Pictures of golf outings with professionals like Sam Snead and Arnold Palmer lined his office walls. When on vacation in the mountains of North Carolina he golfed morning, noon and night, or so it seemed for my patient grandmother. His outgoing and contagious personality entertained the golf caddies throughout the summer months. At one point he found out that one of the young caddies he had gotten to know was having a hard time paying for his college tuition and necessities for college life. Again, without telling anyone he made sure this young man did not have to worry about financial obligations so he could concentrate on his studies.

Finally, my father told a story I could certainly relate to, with my own daughter's onslaught of medical bills. This particular act of kindness involved an extremely ill young girl who needed extensive surgery at Boston Hospital. The family was unable to travel to Boston due to financial hardship. G.G. anonymously set up a trust fund for this young girl so that she and her family could travel to and from Boston for doctor visits. He eventually paid for the surgery itself.

What a testimony for me as I learned of these unselfish acts of kindness. In life, heaps of opportunities abound when we choose generosity as a way of thanking the Lord for the blessings we've been given. The Lord used my grandfather to encourage me to embrace others—in my case, usually without exchanging money—simply by connecting, heart to heart.

A life lesson in... generosity

In reflecting over my grandfather's roundabout way of teaching me about generosity, I believe in some way he trusted me to do the right thing with the money he gave me. There were no stipulations other than don't spend it all in one place. Hopefully, by giving the newly assigned preacher an anonymous gift of cash, it was used in several different ways. Although at times my grandfather seemed to have a heart of a grizzly bear, in reality he had a heart filled with generosity and love for his family and others. In many ways, I believe, he was teaching us to be grateful for the abundance we had been given and it was up to us to make the right choices. Teachers come in all different kinds of packages—my grandfather had to be opened carefully, humbly and respectfully. In the end, he knew where he was going and he felt privileged to be able to help out, whenever there was a need.

Dear Lord, thank You for teachable moments. Thank You for giving us people in our lives to keep us accountable—to help us choose the difference between right and wrong. Thank You for Your example of loving no matter the cost and giving us the greatest gift of all—LOVE—nailed to a cross, forgiving the sins of the whole world.

Amen

"Great opportunities to help others seldom come, but small ones surround us every day."

—Sally Koch, author

"If you can't feed a hundred people, just feed one."

—Mother Teresa, goodwill ambassador, missionary

4

A Blooming Friendship with Jan and M.E.

"Dear friends, let us love one another, for love comes from God. Everyone who loves has been born of God and loves God."

I John 4:7

Recently I was reminded of my best friend Jan's mother. We fondly referred to her as M.E., short for Mary Ellen, and she warmly called me M.A., a lifelong bond I'll always treasure. Several years ago, M.E. unexpectedly went to be with The Lord. She'd undergone a fairly routine outpatient procedure for skin cancer. Afterwards, she went home to rest for a while and never woke up. The news devastated her family and friends. M.E. had been an integral part of her South Florida community. She was a respected and dearly loved wife, mother, friend, church member and . . . gardener.

M.E. loved being outdoors. She wore a familiar wide-brimmed straw hat to protect her skin from the steamy Florida sunshine. When residents of our picturesque neighborhood drove past her home they'd likely see

Mary Ellen, out front, tending her garden. She'd wave thoughtfully and go back to her yard work. The memory of this lovely woman and the deep devotion she held for her family and her favorite things was contagious. I felt blessed to know her and grateful that I too had a lovely mother, just like my best friend.

The day Jan called me with the sad news I still remember feeling numb. *Not our sweet M.E., not now,* I thought. A few days later I headed down south for the funeral from my home in North Florida. I felt an overwhelming sense of sadness, joy and love. Sadness because she'd be missed by so many; joy for the happy times spent with her, and love that bound us together, even today. She loved her children and their friends. Ordinary days were special occasions at their house. Laughter abounded. Hugs were always in order. When I heard her call out "M.A." in her polished southern accent, I felt all was right with the world.

M.E. always made outings extra special. She signed a few lucky second grade girls out of class, for instance, to go watch *Gone with the Wind* for the first time. The private school we attended was quite strict and usually didn't allow such outings, which made the experience even more special. Soon after high school graduation a group of friends were invited over to Jan's house for a photo op. Yes, M.E. stood proudly as our class photographer. "Okay girly girls. Line up on the staircase so we can get a picture of all my girls." There were probably fifteen of us! She beamed with pride reminding us how proud she was of our accomplishment.

One steamy summer afternoon she invited some of Jan's friends over to watch the heart-warming movie, *Brian's Song.* Girls, boys, and sweet M.E. wiped the tears away as we watched two special friends grieve over a terminal illness that brought one friend to an early and quite painful death. The deep love of two friends struck all of us. I believe that's the very thing

M.E. wanted all of us to learn. In the midst of tragedy, the characters' faith stood strong, hope never failed and love abounded.

From watching old movies to attending a grand affair with both of our families, life was never dull when M.E. was around. Like my own mother, she was a bundle of energy and handed out bushels of love to those around her. She tended to life much like she tended to her garden: carefully, with love and devotion, realizing there were thorns, dry spells and broken branches amidst the splendor of her cherished belongings. Her example of unchanging love, her quiet faith and her abounding hope for the world around her was infectious. She raised four children who loved and respected her, giving her the greatest gift of all. They continue to emulate her beautiful life as do their own children, all dedicated to their faith, their family and their community.

At this point I would be remiss if I didn't mention my own mother. Although she was not a gardener, K.K., as most everyone refers to her, walked gracefully among the many thorn bushes and broken branches in her own life. She used the skills of a master gardener to make sure her family was fully immersed in faith, hope, love and doing unto others. From entertaining dignitaries, pregnant teens and homeless people in our gracious guest house to throwing together a barbeque for teenagers at a Young Life Bible study every Monday night, K.K. nourished her budding garden.

She once stated at a Christian Women's Club luncheon, "Before I met the Lord I was on a social merry-go-round that was spinning out of control." Everywhere she looked a broken branch had fallen on her family, a prickly thorn bush had torn her heart in two or a dry spell left her feeling parched and lifeless. Through it all, she smiled. She kept on trudging through the parched and leafless garden, tending things here and there, until finally one tiny rose bud grew and soon sprouted with hundreds of glorious blossoms. Her shining example of taking up the cross and following Jesus no matter what her circumstances gave those around her hope for the future.

Not long ago, after going through my own dry spell (a long illness); I walked out into my backyard which overlooked a sparkling lake and a manicured lawn. I bent down to pick up a watering can I hadn't used in a while and noticed two tiny branches had broken off of my favorite pot of pink geraniums. I set the watering can down beside a lawn chair. *What would Jan's mother have done?* I wondered. I picked up the two fragile, leafless branches and set each one in a separate area of the large ceramic pot. Then I picked up the watering can once again and carefully dampened the branches.

Several days passed—somehow life got in the way of my novice gardening efforts—so I decided it was time to check on my fragile little stems. I bent over hopeful to see a bit of growth. The first branch was still dry and dangling to its side. *Oh well,* I thought, *at least I tried.* Then I glanced over at the second stem, taking in a deep breath. *Oh my goodness, it worked; it actually worked.* Instead of brown and lifeless, two tiny green leaves were attached to the newly transplanted stem. It had actually taken root. I gently pulled on the middle of the stem just to make sure it had grounded itself in the soil. Much to my surprise it had.

Glancing up above the treetops I set my eyes upon the hovering gray clouds. I stretched on my tiptoes as if I could see anything beyond the thick cloud cover! God must have been laughing at my childlike enthusiasm. For the moment, I had forgotten about my balance issues and I lost my sense of space and tumbled. I'm sure the neighbors were wondering what in the world was going on across the lake, but somehow it didn't matter.

I regained my balance and looking up with a smile, I whispered, "Lord, You have an amazing way of opening my eyes." I silently continued my conversation with Him. *This little plant is just like me . . . broken, parched and lifeless and yet there's life in the depths of my soul.* He, in spite of the tippy-toe experience, could see straight into my heart and He knew I needed a strong picture, a symbol of what we are without Him. Simply put the branch that didn't take root. Nearby was the symbol of what we can be when we've given our lives over to Him—the branch that surprisingly came back to life in a few short days.

I had to share my experience with someone. Why not my mother, the one who taught me everything she knew about broken up people and how to mend them back together again. Someone who had become like a second mother to Jan. "Hey darlin'," the voice said on the other end of the phone. "Hey K.K.," I replied. I went on to tell her the story of the broken branch and the healing process it went through and how it reminded me of my life. Her voice sounded a bit choked up as did mine. "Isn't that just like the Looord," she declared in her sweet southern drawl. "Oh honey, what a precious story of God using broken things to show us His strength and mercy in times of adversity."

As for Jan, we still share moments of laughter, tears and brokenness. Our lives are quite different from most of the friends we grew up with. A lot has changed since we used to meet as children halfway between our houses on Christmas morning to show off our favorite gift—usually a beautiful doll to add to our collection. Many years ago Jan's husband lost his high-level job due to "politics" in a large banking institution. I lost my husband in a long, drawn out divorce. None of these trials would have crossed our minds as youngsters. Our charmed lives were something we had been privileged to lead; we knew nothing else. Now the moments we share are just as special; they are just different. We both have daughters with frustrating seizure disorders. Our money no longer grows on trees, and our faith is stronger than it's ever been. That's what keeps us going even on the days when we think we've had enough; but we don't have to worry about that—Jesus is always there to catch us on those not-so-charming days.

The broken branches in my life continue to lead me down a path to extraordinary people; people who have changed my life. People like Jan and her sweet mother. A group of people a lot like you and me.

> ### A life lesson in... friendship
>
> True friends, regardless of their age, interests, or spiritual maturity are a gift from God. He tells us in Proverbs that there is a friend who sticketh closer than a brother. And the Bible tells the beautiful story of Ruth, and her mother-in-law, Naomi, who have a relationship that no man or woman, no time or dwelling place could ever take away from them. They were bound together by unchanging, God-breathed love. Some of us have been given many friends; some of us have been given a few friends who truly make this world a better place to live in. Friends must be nurtured just like our relationship with the Lord. Let us remember to hold those friends close to our hearts and let them know how special they are to us, for we do not know what the future brings. I thank God for friends like Jan and M.E.—for they have shown me even in death, even the miles that keep us apart, that we are connected by a bond that will never end. Friendship is truly a blessing from the Lord.
>
> *Thank You Lord for close friends who love You*
> *and one another...for love is from You.*
>
> *Amen*

"A single rose can be my garden . . . a single friend, my world."
—Leo Buscaglia, American author and speaker

"And the Lord will continually guide you and satisfy your desire in scorched places, and give strength to your bones; and you will be like a watered garden, and like a spring of water whose waters do not fail."
—Isaiah 58:11

5

Learning from Annie

"Blessed be the God and Father of our Lord Jesus Christ,
the Father of mercies and God of all comfort, who comforts us in our
affliction so that we will be able to comfort those
who are in any affliction with the comfort with which we
ourselves are comforted by God."
2 Corinthians 1: 3–4

Years ago I joined a group of women, all with young children at home, who each chose a charitable organization and volunteered once or twice a week. Finding the time wasn't always easy, but I wanted to make the commitment. My first assignment led me to The Day House, an historic greyish-white Georgian residence nestled among giant oaks near the St. John's River in Jacksonville, Florida. It extended meals, light entertainment and support to people with Alzheimer's disease.

I knew little about the disease itself, just enough to feel compassion for the families who watched their loved ones fade away. Sometimes the condition progressed far too fast for the family to care for them without some form of intervention. The Day House provided sought-after relief and more.

The director, a lovely, soft-spoken woman, gave me some pointers and a few cautionary remarks before I met a few of the daytime outpatients. "Are there any particular problems I should be aware of?" I asked. She suggested I watch out for a judge in the program who had a tendency to wander aimlessly.

"Let's see if we can find our wandering judge," she said. Sure enough, the tall, strikingly handsome older gentleman paced around the living room as if he were on a mission. "He has digressed fairly quickly. You just never know how aggressively Alzheimer's will affect a patient."

It took me a moment to regain my composure after witnessing a man, close to my father's age, literally shuffling around in a near mummified state. No emotion, no evident interest in life, just a fixed gaze and a lifeless gait carried him endlessly throughout the living spaces of The Day House.

Then one morning, as my mind raced back and forth over the mountainous list of things I still needed to do later that day, I saw a woman whose name I was told was Annie. She was sitting quietly on a well-used sofa facing a window that looked out over the sprawling oaks and the sparkling river.

"Hello," I said, trying to sound composed. "How are you today?"

The woman nodded her head and smiled pleasantly.

"My name is Mary Ann," I continued. "You must be Annie. I've heard so much about you from the director. You like books, don't you?"

She nodded and smiled in a childlike manner. A worn leather-bound King James Version of the Bible sat comfortably in her lap.

"Would you like to read today?" I asked.

She handed over her treasured copy of the Holy Book. I opened the tattered pages to Psalm 23 and began to read aloud: "The Lord is my shepherd... Surely goodness and mercy shall follow me all the days of my life, and I will dwell in the house of the Lord forever."

Annie took my hand and pulled me over closely to her side. "Again," she pleaded. I don't know how many times I read the 23rd Psalm to Annie in the months I spent at The Day House. I stopped counting after the first day. The truth is, I felt such an unexpected sense of renewal in these moments.

Most of the time, Annie let me know what she needed with simple gestures. She would glance out to the porch and I knew she was ready for a short walk. Sometimes she pointed her finger up toward the sky and smiled; God had given her a beautiful cloudless day to enjoy with the others at The Day House.

Annie's smile and few mumbled words, along with her tender heart, helped us create a special bond. We both clearly loved our family and our God; we connected in a warm and adoring way. Her great capacity to love was evident in her gestures, in her whispers and in her eyes. Many years later, because of her, I was able to accept more readily my beloved grandmother's bewildering state of crossing into Alzheimer's.

Moments with Annie were so memorable. The most unlikely of teachers, she wordlessly taught me a life-changing lesson about simple pleasures. She nurtured in me an appreciation for the simplest of things: daffodils near the house, the river's gurgle, a shared Biblical reading. Through her I came to a renewed sense of God's connectedness uniting us all, no matter our physical or mental state. In the day's hustle and bustle, Annie showed me how pausing to embrace quiet moments can bring joy and calm our restless souls.

More than anything, Annie simply wanted affirmation that someone, anyone, understood and accepted who she had become. The beautiful lesson I learned: in spite of her bewildering condition, the warmth of her eternal love and the tender heart she held close were still intact.

> ## A life lesson in... eternal love
>
> Annie's battle with Alzheimer's disease, much like my grandmother's, seemed to be cruel and relentless when I first met her—not unlike cancer or any other debilitating disease we humans endure. But the more I watched her eyes, her faint smile when we read her favorite verses there was an unmistakable strength in her weakness. A strength that only a loving, merciful God can bestow upon His children when they are in great despair. I believe when Annie stared out the window at The Day House, she was actually gazing into Heaven's Gate. That would explain her childlike smile and the eternal love that flowed from her heart to all those around her. She chose to embrace the grace, the beauty and the love given freely by the very One who created her. Annie was a blessing to me and she will always be....
>
> *Dear Lord, thank You for precious friends we hold dear. You have given us moments of grace and mercy in times of unimaginable pain. Remind us to thank You for these difficult moments—because in thanksgiving we are brought closer to Your throne of grace. Thank You for giving us time with special ones who exemplify Your grace and eternal love. Thank You for the blessings of those who teach us to be more like You.*
>
> *Amen*

"One of the best parts of being human is other humans. It's true, because life is hard; but people get to show up for one another, as God told us to, and we remember we are loved and seen and God is here and we are not alone. We can't deliver folks from their pits, but we sure get in there with them until God does."

—Jen Hatmaker, author

6

Behind Rosie's Smile

"This is the day which the Lord has made;
Let us rejoice and be glad in it."
Psalm 118:24

On a sizzling hot August morning an unfamiliar car pulled into my circular driveway, just three days after our long-awaited son Martin made his entrance into this world. His elated older sisters, Elizabeth and Caroline, thought he was the most amazing play toy they had ever seen.

"I'll get the door, Mommy," announced Elizabeth, my oldest child.

I wondered who might be ringing my doorbell so early in the morning. Gingerly I crept down the stairs and saw a beautiful dark-skinned woman with a radiant smile standing in my entryway. Referring to my mother-in-law, she said, "My name is Rosie. Mrs. Judy suggested I stop by to meet you and the girls, and your fine baby boy. She thought you might need some help with your busy schedule. God bless you all."

"Yes," I said immediately.

My husband traveled for his job almost every week, and I was involved in entertaining clients, volunteering at the girl's school, getting used to a new baby around the house and other motherly duties. Elizabeth's seizure disorder and juvenile arthritis required extra attention and frequent visits to the doctor's office. With my parents living in another town, I knew I could use a stand-in mom who loved children and could help watch the new baby and the girls while I was away from time to time. My mother-in-law had mentioned a woman who needed work, adding that she had strong faith and a heap of patience.

The girls took her by the hand and pulled her up to the second floor nursery. From the floor below I could hear Rosie exclaim, "Oooooh, this is a blessed baby boy. Can I hold him, please?"

"Be very careful," the girls chimed in.

I slowly sneaked up the stairs to check more closely on my newborn's attendants. Rosie held Martin so tightly to her chest I was afraid he might stop breathing, but she obviously knew what she was doing. After all, my mother-in-law mentioned that Rosie had raised her seven siblings after their mother died on a cotton farm in Mississippi, plus five of her own children and numerous grandchildren.

"That is the sweetest child I've ever seen," she said. "Lord knows he's going to be a fine son."

I soon learned Rosie was a saint, spreading goodwill here on earth. Despite her battles with various health issues, children and grandchildren living at various times in her home and a husband who dipped into the bottle more frequently than Rosie would have liked, her ability to rise above her circumstances was remarkable. "I just do what I gotta do with the good Lord's help."

On one afternoon, after Rosie had been working with us for a few years, I went back to my bedroom with Martin, then three, to take a nap. He had a terrible case of croup and when he coughed, a raspy rattle erupted from his chest. He hadn't slept well for several nights and neither had I. Rosie knew he wasn't feeling well and, as I had asked, she came in to check on him after I fell asleep.

"Mary Ann, get up quick, quick now," she said urgently. "This child ain't breathin' very good . . . he's blue. His lips are blue."

I jumped out of bed, gently shaking his lethargic body and pleaded with him to wake up. "Martin, honey, stay with us."

"Mary Ann, just pray," said Rosie. She then repeated over and over, "Thank you Jesus, thank you Jesus for this fine baby boy."

My pediatrician, Dr. Conner, was located only a few short blocks from our house. We rushed Martin into the waiting room and Dr. Conner hurried out to meet us. "We are going to try a breathing treatment with a drug called Albuterol to open up his airways," she said. "If this doesn't work very quickly we'll have to get him to the nearest emergency room."

Five minutes seemed like five hours. Rosie held my hand and I clutched hers while I whispered, "I love you" to my precious little boy. I prayed fervently for more time and more memories with my only son.

Rosie grabbed her purse and looked feverishly inside. She pulled out a glass bottle of olive oil that had been blessed. The doctor looked perplexed, but said nothing. Without a word, Rosie poured a small amount of oil into her hands and rubbed it over Martin's still-lifeless body. "Jesus, heal this baby boy now," she pleaded. "Yes, Lord, thank you for Martin."

The breathing treatments so far were not enough to sufficiently open his tiny airways. The decision was made to transport him to Jacksonville's Beaches Baptist Hospital. A team of doctors and pulmonary specialists met us at the entrance to the ER.

"Who is the mother of this child?"

"We are," I answered anxiously, pointing to Rosie and myself.

The doctor smiled and asked, "You are the child's mother, I assume."

"Oh, yes. I meant we're both like his mother. We both love him."

"Ma'am, your son is going to be just fine."

Rosie raised her hands and uttered, "Thank ya, thank ya Jesus, Lord. Praise your Holy name."

The nurse gave Martin a steroid shot and several breathing treatments. His vital signs began to stabilize and our usually calm three-year-old was suddenly a bundle of energy from the injection. After one last look, the doctor released our brave, much-improved little patient. As we drove home, Rosie sat with Martin in the back seat and she continued to pray.

On a daily basis Rosie's faith taught those around her to reach toward a higher calling. Her songs of praise radiated a sense of hope and love throughout our home, even when she stood silently completing a task.

When rain flooded the yard Rosie exclaimed. "Thank you, Lord."

When her car broke down and the air conditioner no longer blew cold air, her response, "Thank you, Jesus."

When her husband lay lifeless in the ICU with little hope of regaining consciousness, Rosie told the doctors, "Curtis is comin' back. Jesus is bringin' him back to us." Sure enough, several weeks passed and a surprised doctor wrote orders for Curtis to move into a rehab facility. He truly had come back, with a miracle from God and Rosie's great capacity for faith, hope, and love.

Not long ago when "our" only son came home from college for a weekend visit, Rosie asked if we could stop by her house. As we walked in I could see she had chosen the same straw colored paint on her walls as I had used. A hallway displayed family pictures similar to the design we used at our house, and there was some of the furniture I'd given her when we had moved to a smaller home: a large silk flower arrangement sat on a wooden chest that once graced one of our bedrooms. A brass mail sorter and a ceramic lamp with a faded lampshade adorned the antique chest. "You taught me a lot about decoratin', Mary Ann." We hugged one another and smiled.

One of her eleven grandchildren tagged behind her like a newborn puppy. Martin, who was like another one of Rosie's many children, soon caught her up on college life.

Nineteen years have passed since I first met Rosie, a lot of miles of life. Through it all, Rosie has stood beside me and my children. I tell her she is like a mother, a sister, and a best friend all rolled into one. Her commitment to God, her family, her church, The Mighty Church of the Redeemed and people in need is remarkable. Rosie makes life seem like a well-orchestrated symphony, even when there are a few broken strings needing repair.

Sometimes in life we are given the chance to catch a glimpse of a true saint. Rosie's life always reminds me of 1 Corinthian's 13:13, "And now these three remain: faith, hope and love but the greatest of these is love."

"Have you had a kindness shown?
Pass it on;
'Twas not given for thee alone,
Pass it on.
Let it travel down the years,
Let it wipe another's tears,

'Til in heaven the deed appears—pass it on."
—Henry Burton, Methodist minister (1840–1930)

"Joy is found in Jesus when we rejoice in Him. We can rejoice our way to joy."
—George Foster, author

A life lesson in... rejoicing in faith

Whether taking care of grandchildren, singing in the choir, making dinners for her beloved church, taking care of her sickly husband, traveling to Mississippi to visit one of her sisters, or dealing with her own physical ailments, Rosie epitomizes rejoicing in faith. When she talks about the Bible she doesn't simply talk about it, she quotes it word for word—she knows and claims God's promises and walks the walk regardless of her circumstances. She is a saint, an angel and a faithful servant wrapped in a package with a smile that never ends. "Rosie, how do you do it all and never complain?" I ask. "I just think about Jesus hangin' on the cross for me and I just have to praise Him, praise His Holy name." She continues, "You know, He doesn't ask very much of us, only to trust and obey." Rosie takes a deep breath. She raises her weathered hand in the air and grins, "I'm so blessed, child, so very blessed." And you can see the joy on her face.

My mother used to sing us a song by a Swede named Evie Tornquist that reminds me of sweet Rosie, "...And you'll know where I am going by the look on my face... going special delivery... and you'll know where I am goin' by the look on my face." I believe Evie must have known someone like Rosie in her lifetime. I'm blessed to know and love such a lovely, Godly woman. She exemplifies the love of Jesus and the joy of being His child.

Lord bless those who smile in the face of adversity. Thank You that You have called us to encourage one another in love, and praise Your Holy name. Thank You for Your promises that give us hope for our future and teach us to trust You in spite of our circumstances. Thank You for the smiles of Your angels here on earth as they rejoice in Your presence.

Amen

Prescriptions

For Being Real

In Psalms 139:14 the Bible states, "I praise you because I am fearfully and wonderfully made; your works are wonderful, I know that full well." NIV

The Lord wants us to be "real." He made us in His image and we are to praise Him for His handiwork. He created us to be unique, to be ourselves, and nobody else. He knows what we need before we even compose our thoughts toward a certain decision or situation. He gives us a clear choice: to be ourselves, "acting medium," or to be someone we're not. When we thank Him for who we are in Him, blessings flow and our prayers are answered, out of obedience to our faithful Lord.

7

A Prescription from Dr. Swindoll

"For we are His workmanship, created in Christ Jesus for good works, which God prepared beforehand, that we should walk in them."
Ephesians 2:10

Many years ago my mother gave me a book called *The Finishing Touch*, written by a well-respected author and biblical scholar, Dr. Chuck Swindoll. In it, he describes his version of being real: being yourself without conforming to the world's view of who you should be or ought to be. He encourages his readers to "act medium."

"Meaning what?" Dr. Swindoll explains, "Meaning no self-reference to some enviable accomplishment . . . Meaning no desire to manipulate and manufacture praise. Meaning, authentic surprise when being applauded."

He goes on to say, "The answer lies in consistently taking notice of other's achievements, recognizing other's skills and contributions, and saying so. That's called serving others in love."

My mother gave me this thought-provoking book when my husband and I were trying to decide whether to stay in a house the children and I dearly loved or move to a Mediterranean monstrosity with curb appeal. It wasn't simply a move to a new house; it was a reality-check. As a teenager, I had grown up in a prestigious neighborhood where the majority of people, I realized even then, were trying to keep up with the Joneses. For me, in my thirties, I wanted to stay connected to the people in my old neighborhood who brought me and my children joy and a sense of belonging. *What did Jesus want?* I thought. I knew the only way the children and I would be content was to put the decision in His capable hands and see what happened.

Nevertheless, the thought of saying goodbye to Delores, an elderly woman who lived next door with her ailing husband, left me feeling a bit melancholy. Recently retired, this strong-willed and self-reliant cosmetic executive looked forward to our afternoon visits and waited on the lawn for the children to arrive home from school.

Delores counted on my random knocks on her front door to say hello or to catch her up on my kids' progress in school. She was the watchdog of the cul-de-sac and took her job seriously. I would miss her along with my other neighbors and friends.

Realizing that I would be moving away from a home and a way of life I loved left me feeling slightly on edge. Consequently, my mother could see I needed a dose of sound wisdom from a person who had dealt resourcefully with life's unforeseen moments. As I read through the pages of experiences that molded Swindoll into a man of grace, integrity and wisdom, I began to wonder what purpose I served in LIFE!

Swindoll told the story of a group of children who had built a cardboard clubhouse where they could meet and play. One particular excerpt caught my attention. "Because a clubhouse has to have rules, the children came up with three: Nobody act big, nobody act small, everybody act medium."

Despite the immense responsibilities Dr. Swindoll dealt with on a daily basis, he knew there was something more important than his work. As a pastor, a husband and a father he recognized the importance of being "real" and sharing a sense of modesty and humility with others.

This story had a huge impact on me at a time when I was feeling uneasy about being seen as "acting big." I simply wanted to be normal like my friends. I realized the choice was up to me; whether I chose to embrace the needs of others or whether I focused on my own desires. The lesson is simple: Be yourself no matter where life takes you. Life is curious at times, and God certainly has a sense of humor. We did end up moving to the Mediterranean fortress. Interestingly, it became a fortress for my children's friends. They spent lots of time at our home while other kids were out doing "their own thing." God knew, once again, our new house would become a refuge for young teens—and He blessed the friendships of those who spent time with us. They knew they could be themselves, without being judged by others.

Dr. Swindoll's story reminded me of an encounter my mother had with a woman who worked as a cook in the cafeteria while I was attending college in North Carolina. My mother was a fine example of being real. She was visiting friends and attending a women's seminar at a local church, which gave her the opportunity to spend a couple of days with me.

One afternoon mother walked over to the school cafeteria just before closing and asked for an iced tea. The frustrated woman behind the counter shook her head. "Why do people always show up just at the time when I'm ready to go home," she said.

My mother apologized for coming in so late. The woman continued, "I still have all these dishes to wash and things to do before I can leave." Taking off her pale yellow ultra-suede jacket, mother announced she was going to help clean up.

"Oh no, a lady like you can't come back here and help me in this nasty kitchen," said the frustrated woman. "Why would you do such a thing?"

My mother, always herself in any given situation, said in her sweet southern accent, "We are placed on this earth to help and encourage others, and I'd like to encourage you to see the young people you serve as a chance to make a positive difference in their lives."

I am sure the woman looked shocked. She begrudgingly fixed mother's iced tea and said, "I can't let you come back behind the counter. But I would like someone to talk to." They talked for some time about faith in God, believing in yourself and being an example to others. Before long, the woman whose name was Alice asked if my mother would be coming back any time soon.

"As a matter of fact, I'll be back in two weeks for parents' weekend to see my daughter," mother said, "and I'll make sure to stop in earlier next time to get my iced tea and check on how you're doing." Mother told Alice that she would be praying for her every day until her return.

Two weeks later, I met my mother at the cafeteria for iced tea. Alice noticed us standing together in the crowded room. Her countenance was glowing. My mother asked, "How are things going?"

Alice practically gushed with joy. "I feel like a new person. Now I enjoy feeding the students and they see a difference in me. I can see it by the look on their faces."

Once again my mother, being exactly who she always had been, amazed me. She was comfortable with who she was and had a heart for helping others. She was willing to roll up the sleeves of her beautiful silk blouse and reach out with compassion to a woman who simply needed a kind word or deed. Thankfully for Alice's sake, mother was able to "act medium" and, in turn, Alice found a piece of herself she thought she had lost.

Today you can choose to recognize that by being yourself and allowing others to see the real you, you might just leave an "Angel Mark," without even knowing it. Angel Marks are what I like to think of as simple, often unanticipated, moments of pure kindness shared with another person. They bring joy to the hearts of the giver and receiver. I'm sending you one today.

A life lesson in... being yourself

The truth is, I spent most of my life not being myself. I wanted so desperately to be accepted that I ended up in many ways being a great faker! Helping other people was so important to me but I allowed my "standing" in society to get in the way. Every time I was asked to help with a charity event I said, "Yes," without even thinking about it. What I was really thinking: I just want to be me. I just want to help those people who can't really help themselves...broken people—like myself, without the resources to pull themselves up by the bootstraps. It took a painful divorce, a lot of "Heavenly Appointments" with my Father in Heaven and a new perspective on who He wanted me to be, to allow me to see the person God was molding me to be. Stories from Dr. Swindoll and others reminded me that I was exactly who God wanted me to be, as long as I was walking along His divine path, and not my own.

Dear Lord, teach us to be ourselves... After all You made us this way. You want us to be the very children You made to share Your love and Your word with others. Help us to serve others in love—not acting too big or small—simply being ourselves and giving You the glory.

Amen

"Today you are you, that is truer than true. There is no one alive who is youer than you."

—Dr. Seuss, author

"One essential ingredient for being an original, in the day of copies, is courageous vision."

—Charles Swindoll, author, pastor

8

Friendly Reminders from Darby and Ann

"And thou shalt be secure because there is hope."
Job 11:18

My childhood friend Darby called unexpectedly to say hello. A mutual friend of ours mentioned I was a bit "under the weather," a euphemism for my on-going struggle with ulcerative colitis. She could hear my voice was weak and trembling.

We had been friends long enough for her to realize I didn't sound like the same person she had grown up with. After chatting for about an hour Darby suggested I find a babysitter for several days and drive to her home about three hours away for some relaxation. She had no idea how fitting her invitation was at the time.

"Are you sure?" I asked, knowing she had been going through some family-related troubles of her own.

She laughed. "Yes, you know I wouldn't suggest coming here it if I didn't really mean it." I needed help somehow. After being diagnosed with ulcerative colitis, along with being misdiagnosed with several different illnesses, I'd begun to experience severe panic attacks, so severe that I didn't have the strength or energy to properly care for my family. At the time my oldest daughter Lizzy, then eleven, had a chronic seizure disorder, along with juvenile arthritis. Caroline, age nine, was an active, independent child who liked everything to run smoothly. Last but not least Martin, three-years-old, certainly needed the supervision of a mother and desperately craved the attention of his father who was an extremely busy government relations director.

Admitting I needed help was harder than anticipated. After thoughtful consideration, I decided to grab a little down time at Darby's. Fortunately, my mother offered her services to look after the children. She adored her grandchildren and any opportunity to come visit them was a welcome occasion.

Two days later, in mid-October, I arrived at Darby's home. She took one look at my frail one-hundred-pound body and gasped for air. Not quite sure what to say, an unusual dilemma for my lively and vocal friend, she hugged me gently and led me into her kitchen.

"Okay skinny-minny," she finally insisted, "we're going to make sure you get some good food and rest. Then she offered a friendly reminder, "Mary Ann, you're going to make it. Remember what Mrs. Davidson told us in Bible class when we were teenagers, from Psalm 46:1? Always remember God is our strength and our refuge when we're feeling down in the dumps or when life throws us a curve ball."

Not only was I feeling down in the dumps, but my body really felt like it was shutting down. There were days I felt like I needed my own personal restroom around every turn as I struggled with colitis. Too much information! My thyroid was also working overtime (thyroiditis) leaving me anxious and sleep-deprived and my overall health left me virtually defenseless. Even my sense of humor, something Darby and I had shared since we were young girls, had nearly disappeared.

My first night, a real whirlwind, left me breathless: children running to and fro, friends stopping in to say hello, phones ringing off the hook, and a tired husband who wondered when dinner would be on the table. Pulling Darby aside before heading back to the bedroom, I said, "This is all you need to add to your busy life, a friend who is falling apart at the seams."

"Stop it, right now. I'm so glad you decided to drive down to stay with us. Anyway, we're all a little dysfunctional, you know?" That was Darby. Honest, kind and to the point!

The next morning, after dropping off her kids at school, it turned out that she had a special plan in mind for me. Darby knew my lifeless figure needed more than a friendly pat on the back. We went to see a dynamo named Ann.

"Welcome to our home, Mary Ann," Ann said warmly. "Please make yourself comfortable." The mother of six had a sink-load of dishes, her two large retrievers hovering nearby. I must have been ghostly-looking, distant, but I tried occasionally to join in the conversation about Ann's love of cooking. I wasn't trying to be rude; I simply needed some quiet time to reflect and pray.

Ann must have noticed my lack of interest in the conversation. "Why don't you take a look at the lake while we finish cleaning up," said our hostess.

"Thanks for your understanding, Ann," I said softly. "You and Darby are already a life-saver during this frustrating time, and you're helping me, a perfect stranger."

Placing her hand on my shoulder, she added her friendly reminder, "You're Darby's close friend, and we are here for you just as you would be for us. That's what friends do, right?"

I nodded my head and slowly shuffled out the back door to view the lake. I stared at the still, rippling waters. For so long I'd been sick and overwhelmed. For so long I'd felt a pressing need to hold everything together, but my frail shoulders couldn't hold all the turmoil, not when overlaid with an unrealistic "everything is fine" attitude. In this peaceful place, I surrendered. I found myself thanking God for the gift of these two women who were taking time during their hectic lives for me.

I soon saw what centered and energized Ann: her Bible studies taught to a small group of women in her church and neighborhood. Her home library—filled with devotionals, Bible concordances, and teaching material on various books of the Bible—somehow made me feel protected. Ann spoke of the recent Bible study she was teaching called Precept. Hearing who the author was, I felt such a surprise and a sense of homecoming! Precept's intense study of the Bible was written by biblical scholar Kay Arthur, the very same woman who had provided such transformative guidance for me as a teenager. I felt safe, welcome, and hopeful for the first period in quite some time.

Ann suggested we spend the morning reading the Psalms together. She added, "you could end each day by reading them again to help lift your spirits." So that week we read Psalm 4:11, ("In peace I will both lie down and sleep for thou alone oh Lord dost make me to dwell in safety") and Psalm 27:13–14, ("I would have despaired unless I had believed that I would see the goodness of the Lord; in the land of the living. Wait for the Lord . . . Be strong and let your heart take courage"), among many others. Soon I began to experience a small taste of inner peace.

I expressed how their deep faith helped. Their friendly reminders began to sink in. *Step out in faith and recognize that God is in complete control of everything in your life. Remember that He is your strength and refuge in times of trouble and He will never leave or forsake you.*

God was using these compassionate women to encourage me to reestablish my faith and to use the resources set before me. My own feeble impulses, I realized, were hindering my ability to get well. In fact, my sense of pride was delaying the healing process; I still thought I could miraculously fix my health issues and my declining relationship with my husband. Although my heart was in the right place, I was still trying to control the reins of life. Instead, I needed to allow God to allay my fears and lift my broken body and spirit, and lead me toward renewed health. I said to them a bit hesitantly, I've decided to get the medical attention I've been putting off far too long." These two women helped me to see pride can creep into our lives without even being aware of it.

"A step in the right direction, girlfriend," Darby quipped.

During the first couple of days, however, I wasn't exactly sure how to process their selfless acts of friendship. I wanted always to be the one lending a helping hand. Being on the other end was a humbling experience, to say the least!

As the days went on I began to see the effects of my anxious thoughts and my desire to fix my problems on my own. I remembered the verse in Matthew 6:30–34 which states: "But if God so clothes the grass of the field, which is alive today and tomorrow is thrown into the furnace, will He not much more clothe you? You of little faith . . . So do not worry about tomorrow; for tomorrow will care for itself. Each day has enough trouble of its own."

Yes, I thought, it was time for me to step out in faith and hope, seeking help for the sake of my family and my own future. It was time to let Jesus guide my steps.

The seven days I spent with Darby and Ann ended up being one of the most memorable weeks of my life. It wasn't a vacation. It wasn't a girls' night out. It was a collection of eye-opening revelations, these women by my side. Because of them, I made a difficult decision to leave the ones I dearly loved to seek critically needed medical attention. Their timely intervention and loving support led me to the conclusion that getting well started with me, stepping forward in faith.

Acting selflessly comes in many different forms. No one action is any less noteworthy than another. Darby and Ann expected nothing in return except for the true enjoyment and fulfillment of "paying it forward," in a quiet and humble manner for a hurting friend. Their friendly reminders showed me how much they cared and how important trusting in the Lord was for me, for all of us. Their friendship and love gave me hope for new beginnings.

A life lesson in... hope for new beginnings

I look back on my time with Darby and Ann, almost twenty years ago, and still feel very grateful for having two women give up a week of their busy lives for someone who needed their support. It wasn't simply giving up their week—it was being present in the moment, for as long as it took, to help me understand, even in illness and anguish that God was working in my life. And they reminded me that He makes promises that He always keeps. He will never leave or forsake us. He will never give up on His children and He always has a way out for us, if we just believe. And sometimes it takes coming to the absolute end of ourselves for us to see who is in charge and who can ally all of our fears and longings and give us hope for our future.

Thank You God, for placing people along our path who love You and who are willing to give of their time and energy for your sake. Bless those Lord who bless others. And thank You for opening the way before us, a new beginning, even when we feel completely lost.

Amen

"And if you faithfully obey the voice of the Lord your God, being careful to do all his commandments that I command you today, the Lord your God will set you high above all the nations of the earth."

—Deuteronomy 28:1

"If I can stop one heart from breaking; I shall not live in vain, If I can ease one life the aching, or cure one paining, or help one fainting robin up to its nest again, I shall not live in vain."

—Emily Dickinson, poet

Permission Slip For Healing

Give it all to Jesus:

Fear

Wounded Hearts

Broken Dreams

Illness

Relationships

Temptation

9

Doctor A's Permission Slip

"But now, Lord, for what do I look for? My hope is in you."
Psalm 39:7

In October, soon after my visit with Darby and Ann, I left my home in North Florida, my three wonderful children and a concerned, highly driven, workaholic husband, to meet with an established physician in South Florida. My parents had suggested I see this highly respected physician in my hometown. My weight had continued to drop down to well under one hundred pounds in just over one month, and at five feet six inches, that was too low! In all, I'd lost twenty to thirty pounds. My blood sugar levels would skyrocket and then drop too quickly for my body to compensate. The result: headaches, dizziness, and sometimes fainting spells. The children were scared, my husband was overwhelmed and my anxiety attacks were continuing. I was a mess in need of a major clean up.

I had forgotten what energy looked or felt like. However, my first reaction to my parent's idea wasn't positive. I can't take time off to go so far away, I'd thought. Who would take care of my children? Besides, part of me still held onto the notion that my health problems would fix themselves, but I decided to go. Still, I couldn't quite bring myself to voicing the helplessness I felt as picked up the phone to call my mother. The voicemail answered so I decided to leave a brief, general message.

"Mother," I began, trying to sound nonchalant. "I could really use your help right now, and you'll have the chance to spend some quality time with your grandchildren." She called right back. "Your father and I are on our way."

Surprisingly, I felt relieved. I knew I couldn't continue on this path much longer. My body was falling apart, both physically and emotionally, even though I thought I had done a pretty good job at hiding my illness from my family. Evidently I had not. They no longer believed I had a simple case of the stomach flu. My parents thought I was actually dying. My husband didn't have time to care for the wife unraveling before him and our children.

Thankfully, the children thought I was going away for an extended vacation while K.K., their adoring grandmother, came to visit. Naively, I imagined I would only be away for a few days. As my father placed my bags in his car, I hugged my children and my husband goodbye. I felt very sad but somehow I knew this was for the best. The near four-hour drive down south, however, seemed like an eternity. *Would I ever feel normal again*, I wondered.

Finally, we arrived. My father grabbed my hand to help me out of the car. A slight breeze brushed through my thinning hair. I gazed up at the stars. Oh please God, I prayed. Help me to get well . . . and can you please make it sooner rather than later, Lord? Of course, I knew the request I'd made was up to Him—but He tells us to pray without ceasing . . . for all things, so I did.

The following morning my father insisted, "We have dinner plans tonight at six and your doctor's appointment is set for tomorrow at 10:00

A.M." What I thought would be a quiet time with my father turned into a three-hour business dinner at a local hotel ballroom. A speaker addressed the audience. I can't recall the theme of his speech, much less his name or what he even looked like. Prior to my panic-ridden life I prided myself on remembering people, places, and details, but on that particular evening, like so many others during that time, my sense of reality was clouded by a state of panic. I leaned over to my father and pleaded, "I have to go now."

The room began to spin, my heart pounded like a racehorse, and I had an overwhelming feeling of helplessness. Looking slightly frustrated, my dad whispered, "I'll meet you outside the ballroom."

I walked sluggishly toward the glass-paned doorway. I wanted to run, but my body felt completely limp. Fear and panic left me nearly motionless. My father walked toward me and put his hand gently on my shoulder. He knew this was not the daughter he was used to. He clutched my hand and smiled, "Mary, let's take a walk."

All I could do was to stare out over the moonlit bay. "Please take me back to your house," I begged. "I don't have the strength to walk or enjoy the evening."

I could feel his frustration and his compassion at the same time. He knew something was desperately wrong and he felt helpless too—but not hopeless. He knew there was hope, even if I didn't at the time. That night I could barely climb under the covers of the sturdy iron bed in the guest room. My slight frame felt suffocated by all the pillows. The drapes were pulled back and the moon's reflection danced upon the shadowy water of the bay. For another guest, the sight would have been breathtaking. For me, it was just a reminder of a long, lonely night ahead.

"Dear God, please help me get well, for the sake of the ones I love." I prayed for my children and my family, thanking Him for my blessings and then held on for dear life.

I'm not sure I slept at all that night, but I thanked God I had made it to another day. He tells us to be thankful in all things and I wanted Him to know I was thankful in spite of my circumstances. Although the sky looked overcast and rain drizzled down, I could see a cargo ship passing by and somehow it seemed, well, beautiful. For a moment I actually felt a fleeting flash of emotion ... not completely numb. *Could there be hope for me?* I thought.

Dragging my emaciated body out of bed, I eased myself toward the dressing room, and stared at my thin hair in the mirror. I wished the person reflected would simply go away, never to return. After a steamy, hot shower my body still shook with chills. Truthfully, I was excited and nervous at the same time about my first appointment with Dr. A. I picked out a tailored form-fitting navy dress and slid into my favorite suede loafers.

"Mary, time to go." my father called.

"Coming, Dad."

We walked down the steps to the parking garage. I got in the car and took a deep breath. "Mary, don't worry; everything is going to be all right." It was about a fifteen-minute drive to the medical center. Both of us were quiet.

A trim, slightly bald, fiftyish man greeted us at the door. "Hello," he said. "You must be Mary Ann." I wanted to say I'm not sure who I am, but I thought better of it. My father went into the waiting room and I was led to a comfortable, over-sized couch. About five feet in front of me, Dr. A. sat down in his swivel chair, folded his hands, blinked his eyes and cleared his throat. He spoke for a while and I listened—for one hour! I gave a nod once in a while, and that was about it.

"I'll see you again in the morning, 10 o'clock."

I nodded my head, and muttered, "thank you."

My homework for the night, as Dr. A suggested: "Try to breathe, Mary Ann, and think of a word that might help you relax." I chose the word, peace. It was the state of being I most longed for, a state we certainly all yearn for in our lifetime. It was only 11 A.M. and I was already exhausted. Was this really worth it, I thought.

The following morning I drove myself to Dr. A's office, which was a major feat in itself. Approximately three weeks had passed since I had driven a car. My life before my illness revolved around my SUV, driving back and forth to school, volunteer activities, grocery store, ballet lessons, basketball, and so on. Driving was a necessity with three young children.

Breathe, just breathe, I reminded myself, slowly navigating along the roads.

For the next three weeks my routine became almost robotic: Drive to Dr. A's office, eat lunch (mostly shaved turkey and mashed potatoes), call my kids, breathe, write in my journal, breathe, dinner (more turkey and potatoes . . . yikes), call the kids to say goodnight, breathe, pray and try to sleep.

After about three to four weeks of seeing Dr. A, he suggested I go back to my parent's house and look into the same mirror I had peered into earlier in the month. There was a catch to this request. Instead of looking in the mirror and seeing a malnourished, frightened individual, Dr. A suggested that I should get angry!

Angry, I thought. *I never get angry.* That was a difficult request for someone who pretended, even in the worst of circumstances, that everything was fine. I could literally be passed out on the floor and tell people around me, "I'm fine; no really, I'm fine."

Well, not this time.

"Stand in front of the mirror and get mad, Mary Ann," he instructed. "Tell yourself that you are tired of being sick, tired of living in panic and tired of not standing up for yourself."

Dr. A told me to let him know when I was really mad! Admittedly, this assignment took several tries. Each time I reported in, he insisted I wasn't really mad. "You're not mad enough yet," he'd say. "Oh dear Lord," I prayed. "Please let me get mad at my illness so I can get back to my family. I give this all to you—that you might be glorified in my weakness."

On the fourth or fifth day, I started feeling upset. I began to think about my children at home without me; I pictured the effects of a less than perfect marriage, the friends I had not seen in weeks, the events I missed with the kids, and the more I thought about it, the more anger I felt. I allowed myself to get really mad! Soon after, I realized Jesus was all I needed at that moment. He held the key to my healing and my life.

The next morning driving to the medical center, I found myself suddenly singing, "Raindrops on roses and whiskers on kittens." It was a song from *The Sound of Music*, which the kids and I watched over and over. That morning I began to remember my favorite things.

I couldn't contain myself at his office. "I'm upset," I began. "I'm mad. I don't want to live like this anymore. My children need me and I'm ready to go home. I've missed my Bible study, too." Dr. A's eyes opened quite wide. I'm not sure he knew how to react to that statement. For me, it was a sign of healing. The Lord heard my prayer. He instilled the faith and the strength within me to stand up and say, *"Enough." It's time for me to go home and be with my family.*

At that moment, I realized that through God's grace a man I knew very little about had given me what amounted to a permission slip to get well. He allowed me to figure out exactly what I needed and that was my family and my God. His professionalism, his perseverance and his kindness helped lead me back to the life I deeply missed. He bestowed the gift of hope and healing on me, a gift I could never repay. Much like the gift we've been given so freely by Jesus, the gift of eternal life—freeing us from a life of sin, worry and pain.

Once again, hope filled my heart and home was only a short drive away, and this time Jesus was steering the wheel.

A life lesson in... healing

Isn't it difficult sometimes to accept things just as they are without asking God, "Why, Lord? Why me?" I'm sure many of us can relate to this all-too-human line of questioning. Over and over He tells us to trust in Him, to have faith and hope in His plans for our lives, even when it hurts. Who knows better what hurt feels like than Jesus? No one. Despite traumatic events that take our breath away; watching a child go to be with the Lord when life has barely begun, seeing a parent with a terminal disease or a friend whose life is spiraling out of control, God is there. And that's the very place where He meets His children and can heal them. The burden-bearer stands ready to wrap His loving arms around us and say, "Be still and know that I am God. I will never leave or forsake you.... I am with you even until the ends of the earth." What a relief. What an amazing gift if we choose to accept that He will be there waiting and watching because he's gone through the toughest of times and He knows our hurt and pain better than anyone.

Dear Lord, please give us the hope we need for healing as we walk through the unexpected detours of life. Let Your footprints remind us that You know where we've been and where we're going. And that You've already gone before us. Grant us peace and joy in the midst of our not-so-easy days. Let us learn to thank You for those times, and learn what You are teaching us through our difficulties. Thank You, Lord.

Amen

"What gives me the most hope every day is God's grace, knowing that His grace is going to give me the strength whatever I face, knowing that nothing is a surprise to God."

—Rick Warren, pastor, motivational speaker

"Our wounds are often the openings into the best and most beautiful part of us."

—David Richo, speaker

10

The Tennessee Trucker

"And do not forget to do good and to share with others,
for with such sacrifices God is pleased."
Hebrews 13:16

After school let out for the summer, I would pack my children and a few of their friends into my station wagon and head to my parents' mountain-top getaway in North Carolina. One unforgettable Sunday morning I set out with my three children and two of their friends—four girls and one boy, my youngest to be exact.

Fortunately, my son, then six, was busy playing with his new Gameboy, and he hardly even noticed he was stuck in a car with so many women! The Indians were beginning to get a bit restless, so after two hours of driving I decided to pull over at Exit 101, a truck stop in Cordele, Georgia, that offered several different dining options for the kids.

What happened next is hard for me to admit. After all, I had been given a certificate by a Range Rover School for making a "10 out of 10" on their rough terrain course in West Virginia. For a brief moment I must have forgotten that I was driving a Volvo station wagon and not an all-terrain vehicle. I turned on my left blinker to enter the truck stop's large parking lot, and just as I was making a practically perfect turn, I looked back to say something to the children. Big mistake!

I heard the kids squeal. "Mom, watch out!" It was too late. Somehow my excellent driving skills hurled us over a concrete median separating the entrance and exit to the truck stop. Actually, we didn't quite make it over. We were anchored on top of the median with the front end of my car leaning forward.

With so many children in the car I had to stay calm. I told them to stay inside and I would check out the situation. By the time I climbed out and hopped over the median I began to smell gas. "Everybody out quick," I said, as calmly as possible. "Let's get some lunch."

The girls walked their younger brother across the parking lot into the restaurant. Peering at us from across the parking lot, a group of well-dressed, bulky young men jumped out of their pickup truck and sprinted over. One guy pushed and pulled at the Volvo and grunted to the point I finally had to ask him to stop.

Gently moving through the others, a heavier young man pushed up his sleeves and said, "I got this." In one fell swoop, the man (with his Sunday suit on) placed his hands under the front end of my car, took a deep breath and heaved the station wagon over the median and onto the level pavement behind us. I was speechless. To this day I still wonder if that young man is playing as a linebacker on a field somewhere for the National Football League!

Without even thinking, I opened my purse, grabbed as much cash as I could and handed the money to him. "Please," I said, "take this as a small token of my appreciation."

"Oh, that isn't necessary."

"Oh, please, lunch and dinner is on me," I replied. God bless you."

One of the mechanics towed my car back to the service area and I went inside to eat with the kids. The girls were a little teary-eyed and my son was still playing with his Gameboy, as if nothing happened. "Let's get lunch," I told them, "and then we'll check on the car."

A nice waitress took our order and brought the food back promptly. We bowed our heads, said the blessing and finished our lunch in no time. What I thought might be an hour or so; however, turned into about five.

We got to know just about everyone. One truck driver, for instance, wore a cowboy hat and looked like he was taking a nap most of the time. Late in the afternoon, he headed toward our table. "Hello there, ma'am," he said in a deep Southern drawl. "I noticed you have been here for quite some time."

"Yes, we have a bit of a car issue," I replied.

My Caroline announced, "Mommy drove over a big piece of concrete and we got stuck." There went my perfect driving record, down the drain, again.

"I noticed you said a blessin' with yer kids and it reminded me of my family back home in Tennessee," the trucker began. He'd never forget, he said, seeing five children act so gracious and respectful in spite of the events of the day. "If I can be of any assistance, please let me know. I sure wouldn't want my family stuck in a truck stop all night."

We thanked him and said our goodbyes. Soon the mechanic found us in the dining area and told us our ruptured fuel line was fixed as far as he could tell. I wasn't completely convinced, and I don't think he was either. It was almost eight P.M., and we had another four hours to drive. "Let's get going," I said to the kids. "We have to get to the mountains."

Making sure to go around the median this time, I hopped on I-75 heading north toward Atlanta. After about five minutes my daughter Elizabeth said she smelled gasoline. I stopped immediately on the shoulder and carefully got out. She was right. Gas was leaking quickly from underneath the car. *What now?* I thought.

It was by now almost nine o'clock at night, and I had five tired kids standing in a ditch several feet away from the car. Tears were beginning to form in my eyes. Suddenly, I was startled by the resounding boom of a truck horn. "Oh great, now we're going to be run over by a semi," said my daughter's friend with a nervous laugh.

Before I could even say a word, the eighteen-wheeler pulled in right behind us. A tall, slender, familiar looking man hopped down from his cab. "Ma'am, don't be alarmed," he said.

Of course I was alarmed. It was late at night, my car was leaking gasoline and I had a group of slightly cranky children thinking they were about to be crushed by a semi.

Suddenly, I felt complete inner peace. I had put my trust in the Lord, and it was time I trusted the driver too. The Lord had obviously placed the gentle man at the truck stop for a reason. He is well aware of our needs … it's up to us to trust Him. When my eyes finally focused, I realized the trucker was the same man we'd met at the truck stop. He made a choice to follow us, knowing we might need some help. I wanted to give him a hug, but I didn't.

"Ma'am, we need your car towed to the nearest auto shop," he said. "There happens to be one about a mile up the road." It felt like a miracle. The towing service came and picked up my car. Now what?

Meanwhile, the Tennessee Trucker, as I came to call him, pulled out his wallet and showed me pictures of his beautiful family. "I can help you and your kids to Atlanta," he continued, "so you will be safe and your family can pick you up in the morning."

I really had no choice. I closed my eyes and prayed. "God protect us, and thank you for this unexpected stranger."

He helped the children climb into his roomy cab. My middle daughter asked, "Mommy can we get one of these?" They'd never experienced anything quite so exciting. The kids settled in front of the television, sitting comfortably on the pink shag carpeting as I climbed into the co-pilot seat. As he closed my door, he pulled out a pack of cigarettes and said, "Excuse me ma'am, would ya care for a Camel?" Could this be one of those hidden-camera TV shows, I wondered, and we were being filmed? "No thanks," I said, "I'm fine." The Tennessee Trucker climbed back into his seat, honked his horn, and turned on his blinker to re-enter traffic and off we went.

I have had many amazing journeys in my life, but our time with The Tennessee Trucker (and earlier help from the others at the truck stop) made quite an impression on my entire family. On a not-so-ordinary Sunday afternoon, we had the privilege of experiencing an Appointed Moment, a most surprising occurrence, exactly when we so urgently needed it. I will never forget such kindness and generosity from this Tennessee cowboy. We were safely delivered to a hotel in Atlanta by this unselfish man. At check-in the receptionist asked if the gentleman would be joining us. "No," I said, with a giggle. "Today we were rescued by this real life hero and now he's headed home to Tennessee." We said our goodbyes as the trucker stood and prayed for the safety of a mother and her children. This was a day in the life of a few of God's children that will never be forgotten.

Each time I pass through Georgia (Exit 101), I fondly remember that long summer day that confirmed to me the fact that people who help others tend to help others, again and again! God's gift of Appointed Moments, those moments that come when we least expect them, reminds me of who leads us down the highway of life, always providing light in the darkness and calm amidst the storm—sometimes in the form of a perfect stranger.

A life lesson in... helping strangers

My family and I will always remember the Tennessee Trucker. So many lessons can be learned from this story—the main ones: faith and kindness. Faith that the Lord would protect me, my children and their friends on a dark, dimly lit interstate in the middle of nowhere. Faith that my car would not blow up on the side of the road due to leaking gas. And faith that He was going to get us out of the situation which was causing a great deal of anxiety. He didn't allow us to dwell too long on the pity party because He knew just what we needed. Instead of a policeman or a sheriff or some type of emergency vehicle, The Lord chose a humble trucker who loved God and his family. And... the extremely loud horn on his very large semi to deliver His message. After the initial shock, we all connected to this kind-hearted man. God gave me complete peace as my family back in Florida urged me to change my mind. I had a choice: stay on the side of the interstate with five tired children for who knows how long, not to mention the leaking gas, or trust the Lord and the highly unusual Appointed Moment that led us to a safe hotel and eventually to my parents' home. Although the day was long and my car ended up having to be traded in, the kindness we received from strangers was truly miraculous and God was in complete control—as always!

Dear God, thank You for the people You place along our path; even strangers, who remind us You are in charge.

Amen

"If a man be gracious and courteous to strangers, it shows he is a citizen of the world, and that his heart is no island cut off from other lands, but a continent that joins them."

—Sir Francis Bacon, English statesman, author

"No one is useless in this world who lightens the burdens of another."

—Charles Dickens, author

11

The Silent Angel

*"The steps of a man are established by the Lord,
when he delights in his way..."*
Psalm 37:23

Several years ago my parents were visiting their mountain-top home in North Carolina, about four hours west of Charlotte. My mother drove down the winding road from their house to the town's charming Main Street. Walking down the familiar sidewalk, mother ran into a couple vacationing from Kentucky.

After visiting for quite some time, my mother invited them to come over for refreshments later that evening. This was not unusual for my mother. Zee and Don arrived promptly at six; the two couples immediately bonded. Zee, a decorator and antique dealer, commented on my mother's sense of style. Don and my father discussed their similar business interests. Mom showed Zee around the house while the men made themselves comfortable on the porch.

"These are my four children," said mother. Pictures of our childhood sat displayed among her favorite porcelain pieces in the room.

"Who is this?" asked Zee. She pointed to a picture of me at Queens College in Charlotte. "My twins had a friend at Queens who came to visit us in Lexington and her name was Mary Ann. "And she looks exactly like your daughter. They too could be twins."

Mom exclaimed, "Your girls are Cathy and Ginny?"

"Oh, my goodness," said Zee. "Yes! Can you believe it after all of these years?" Tears began to trickle down their faces.

It seems these Appointed Moments have always been part of my family heritage. Obviously we cannot always explain these extraordinary coincidences or "sparkles of pixie dust," as Caroline, my middle child, light-heartedly describes them. They just seem to happen. I suppose in some cases it is what we expect, or more directly, what we don't expect that leaves these moments of God's grace at our doorstep.

I had first met Cathy and Ginny at The Childhood Education Center at Queens College. In some divine way I believe the same grace and hospitality my mother showed others when we were young led me to them. That encounter led me to an unexpected meeting with a beautiful five-year-old girl at the Childhood Center.

I'd just entered the red brick building on my first day volunteering, and I had great expectations. I liked working with children; their innocence and enthusiasm were refreshing. What I didn't expect was a tall, thin, blonde-haired beauty sitting motionless at a school desk. I placed my hand on her shoulder and bent down to introduce myself. She stared straight ahead as if I were invisible.

I sat beside her and began to draw a picture of a frog on a lily pad. She watched with virtually no emotion. As I colored in the outline of the lily pad, I noticed the little girl began to rock back and forth ever so slightly. She didn't look upset or bored. She simply wasn't focused on anything. To my surprise, she apparently didn't speak.

I asked her questions about her favorite things, her house, her favorite book, her favorite movie. She didn't reply to anything I said or did. She simply continued the rocking motion, and every once in a while she bleated out a slight squealing sound. The two hours I spent with her in some ways seemed like an eternity and yet, somehow, I felt a connection.

The next time at the Childhood Center, I went straight to the director. She explained the young girl had a severe case of autism and she rarely, if ever, spoke, not even a word. Being young and naïve, I couldn't imagine such a lovely child being unable to carry on a conversation. The more time I spent, the more emotionally involved I became. I wanted to meet her parents. I wanted to take her to a doctor. I wanted this disorder to go away. Unfortunately, that was not up to me. It took several months before I actually dealt with the fact this precious child could not express her feelings through conversation, and that I could not really change that.

She began stacking blocks with me after a couple of weeks and would smile briefly once in a while. I slowly learned about her likes and dislikes, and how to keep her on task to some degree. Over time, the quiet and princess-like young girl became my silent angel. Without knowing it, she also prepared me for what I discovered nearly thirty years later.

At that time a cognitive specialist diagnosed my then sixteen-year-old son with Asperger's Syndrome, a high-functioning form of autism that causes the individual to withdraw from social situations, especially with their peers. When the doctor initially discussed his thoughts regarding my often-quiet son, I immediately remembered my first experience with a silent angel. I could literally see her sitting at the school desk.

Once again God had written a script that was unfolding before my eyes in the life of my only son. All of us have been given these Appointed Moments during the course of our lifetime. The question is simply, do we choose to embrace and recognize these moments for what they are?

Whether we refer to them as divine encounters, serendipity, or even an unlikely coincidence, I am grateful and humbled by mine.

There are times I wonder where that special little girl is now and what she might be doing. I would thank her for the memories we made together so many years ago. I would tell her those memories helped prepare me for the unexpected. After the initial shock, I was able to look back and thank the Lord for giving me the privilege of meeting her and my friends Cathy and Ginny. My time at the Childhood Center was divinely appointed, I have no doubt.

Now I look at my amazing son, who has become an independent and quite exemplary young man, with a heart of thankfulness. I thank God for trusting me to raise him. I thank Him for the first silent angel He sent along my path, and for the second one who is now finding his own divinely unique path—a path where God's love directs his every step.

"Every action in our lives touches on some chord that will vibrate in Eternity."
—Edwin Hubbel Chapin, author

"There needs to be a lot more emphasis on what a child can do instead of what he cannot do."
—Temple Grandin, teacher, author, activist for Autism

"Today give a stranger one of your smiles: it might be the only sunshine he (she) sees all day."
—H. Jackson Brown, author

A life lesson in... God directing our steps

The Silent Angel is obviously near and dear to my heart for several reasons. First, God knew on the day a bleary-eyed freshman with a ponytail and a madras skirt stepped out of her parent's station wagon that she (me) had no idea what to expect of college life. I'd been sheltered my entire life, even from hurt and pain for the most part. Second, He knew that I needed someone to teach me about growing up and giving up my own desires for the good of another. And lastly, He knew that teenager would one day be able to accept the news of her son's diagnosis with grace and not bitterness. He knew that I had some growing up to do and it started, ironically, at the Childhood Center. I'd never hurt; really hurt for a complete stranger, for at the time I knew no strangers, only the people in my charmed little world. The Lord's amazing grace gave me a gift without me having any idea what that gift was. He taught me through that first silent angel to embrace with love and devotion my precious second silent angel, my son.

Dear Lord, thank You for going before us when we have no idea where You are taking us. Thank You for hiding us under Your wings until it is the perfect time to let us go and find our way with Your love and guidance. Thank You for giving us what we need at the exact time we need it.

Amen

12

To India, With Love

> "And you shall love the Lord your God with all your heart and with all your soul and with all your mind and with all your strength. The second is this: You shall love your neighbor as yourself. There is no other commandment greater than these."
> Mark 12:30–31

Twenty years ago my family and I moved from an established, sought-after neighborhood in North Florida, to a more casual lifestyle in nearby Ponte Vedra Beach, a family-friendly community known for its beautiful beaches.

Soon after our move, we decided to host a large gathering for the Florida-Georgia football game. Just minutes away in a small shopping center, was a beverage store. I walked in and introduced myself. The owner was a sociable, dark-headed, olive-skinned man with a thick accent. His three small children stood in back of him peering out from the check-out counter. I explained we were new in town.

"I'm not a drinker," I told him, "but we are having a gathering for a sizable group of devoted football fans and I could use your help."

He laughed. "Dat funny, I work here, but I no drink eeder."

I followed a few of his words. He mentioned he was not born in America but he was so happy to live in the United States. "My wife and me from India," he explained. "A very long way from my home."

I couldn't imagine growing up in India and I felt blessed to be an American, as did the hard-working shop owner. "India," I said, using his nickname, "can you help me choose some beverages for my party? I have no idea how much I need or what I should buy."

"No problem, ma'am," he replied. He started to gather bottles and cases of beverages, enough to give me a headache just watching.

"How much do you think this is going to cost?" I inquired uneasily.

"We a little more expensive," India admitted. "But I give you a good deal and I take care of you." I handed over my credit card and signed the receipt.

"Nice to meet you, India!"

"You too ma'am. God bless you."

Through the years I ended up seeing India more than I had originally expected. He always had a smile on his face and always said "God bless you" when I left. Sometimes I walked in the store and he was balanced on one leg, arms out to his side doing stretches. Other times he settled himself on the hard tile floor doing leg lifts or sit-ups.

"Dis is the only time I got to do dis," he would say, slightly embarrassed. "I'm sorry."

"No problem, India," I replied. "It's just as important to take care of your heart as it is to care for your customers."

One afternoon, after a long day in the sun, I ran in to the store to pick up a Gatorade for one of my kids and a bottle of water for me. "How are you?" I asked. "Fine, thank you," India replied. "I a little busy right now.

I leavin' with my family for a trip to India. We be gone two months." He held up two fingers.

That's a very long time, I thought. "Who takes your place for that long?"

"Oh, no problem, I got dat all worked out," he assured me. Then he continued, "I do dis when I can, to help the people in my town. They very poor and when you have money, you have to give it away to help people who need it. We build schools, fix de water pumps, take care of my uncle's air conditioner, and do whatever we can. Now I also tryin' to save some money for young girls who are wantin' to git married because it so expensive to git married over der."

"It must be very expensive to take your entire family overseas." I said.

"Oh yes, very, very expensive." Gesturing with his weathered hands, he explained, "I work the whole year nonstop so I can stay two months. It cost me over $50,000 to help out der."

"India, you are my hero," I said.

How wonderful to learn from others. This humble merchant reminds me of a well-known author, speaker and teacher named Ravi Zachariah who in *Walking from East to West* said about his many returns to his native India: "Sharing with these people some of what I have and seeing the small bit of happiness it brings into their lives is the privilege of a native son." My friend India was forever thinking about how he could improve the lives of his people.

As I started to exit the store, he smiled, looked down at the floor and then clapped his hands together. "You know dis is what I have to do. When we have been given all dis, we need to build something more." It was a reminder of my parent's charge to help others. Then India said something I'll never forget. "Dat is what God want us to do, and nobody has to know what I do. I just like to be invisible."

What an honor to know this generous, kind-hearted man with a heart exemplifying the love of Jesus. I'll remember his humble smile and when he clasps his hands in joy, whispering, "Thank you Jesus for dis' day."

A life lesson in... giving

India will always remind me of the importance of giving back, regardless of the size of our bank accounts. His commitment to honor his family and his homeland has taught me to appreciate the enormous blessings we have been given in our homeland. And let this be a reminder to pray constantly for our authority in government, in our workplaces, in our homes. India is a glowing example of doing unto others as God would have us do. He is well aware that God blesses those who bless others when giving love in time of need. India inspires me in so many ways. "We so blessed here and sometimes people don't even know how blessed we truly is because they never visited my people. My people in India so very poor and de smile when de see someone from our great country come to visit." He adds, shaking his head, "they just don't know, but He know," pointing to Heaven. You're right, I thought. He knows because He is the all-knowing Father.

Dear God, let us give out of the abundance of our hearts and let our light so shine before men that they see You in us.

Amen

"We cannot live only for ourselves. A thousand fibers connect us with our fellow men."

—Herman Melville, author

"The great use of life is to spend it for something that outlasts it."

—William James, American philosopher (1842–1910)

"Are not all angels ministering spirits sent to serve those who will inherit salvation?"

—Hebrews 1:14

13

Joshua and the Darkest Night

*"Fear not, for I am with you; be not dismayed, for I am your God;
I will strengthen you, I will help you, I will uphold you
with my righteous hand."*
Isaiah 41:10

The pre-school my toe-headed, three-year-old son attended was having its annual fund-raising gala. Hundreds of guests would soon line up to bid on a wide range of items, from exotic vacations to stepping stools, hand-painted by their youngsters. We lived only a few blocks away from the beach, and I knew our little man's glossy white stool with brightly colored fish on top had been painted with love.

Earlier in the week I had stopped by his classroom and "accidentally" saw him working diligently on his masterpiece. I wanted to bid on it, regardless of the price!

On the evening of the event my husband had a late business meeting, and we were already running slightly behind. Luckily, we only had about one mile or less to travel, and it was a straight shot down a dimly lit, but familiar road.

We were about two blocks away when I noticed something sprawled out in the middle of the street. "We have to stop." I pleaded. I knew God had placed us there for a reason—I just didn't know why. "We're in a hurry, Mary Ann," my husband said, but he pulled into a nearby shopping center where I started to open the car door before we even came to a complete stop. Frequent roadside stops had become a familiar occurrence, and he wasn't exactly thrilled with the notion.

"What if that were one of our children laid out in the street and no one was around to help?" I insisted. "What would Jesus do, I asked?" He nodded his head in agreement. "Thank you," I said, as I fumbled my way out of the car. I ran to the middle of the street. Until I stepped closer I still thought the small, lifeless shape might be an injured animal.

Stretched out across the dark pavement was . . . a child, a young boy. I crouched over the motionless figure. Gasping for air, I prayed for courage and wept for his parents. Moving closer, I saw he was handsome and blonde-haired, breathless and all alone. His youthful crown had sustained extensive trauma, and blood covered the ground below him. Other than the sizeable wound on the back of his head, he appeared amazingly peaceful, protected seemingly by his garnet and gold football jacket.

On the far side of the road sat an idling station wagon with a woman inside slumped over her steering wheel, wailing. I didn't know who to comfort first, but the child obviously needed immediate attention until an ambulance could arrive.

I placed my hand over his small frame and again prayed. All I could see was the face of a child who could have been my own. His mother likely thought he would be right back home.

People started to gather in the nearby subdivision when the sound of an ambulance grew closer and closer. Across the street a woman with her hand over her mouth charged in our direction screaming, "Please don't let it be my baby, please no."

A parent's worst nightmare was unfolding before my eyes. I kissed the lifeless, fair-skinned boy on the cheek and told him not to be scared. By the time the ambulance arrived, there was no pulse and no life. Slowly, sadly, backing away, I opened the way for the EMT attendants. I was told he felt no pain.

Feeling a profound sense of disbelief, I walked tentatively toward the frightened woman in the car. She was shaking desperately and trying to explain to a police officer that this sweet and innocent child had darted in front of her car without warning.

"There was no time to stop," she explained. "No time to stop. It was dark. He was just too fast and, and. . . ."

I clasped her cold hands in mine and told her I would be praying for her each day. She turned out to be a local school teacher whose world would be forever changed by this tragic event. Later in the evening I found out that the boy, a nine-year-old named Joshua, had been given permission for the first time to carefully cross the street and to go into the local grocery to buy a gallon of milk for his mother.

Somehow my husband and I made it to the last few minutes of the auction simply to pick up our son's masterpiece. We left soon afterwards. As we pulled into our driveway, I pushed the remote control repeatedly to open the garage door. It wouldn't open fast enough.

I raced up the back staircase to peek in on my three beautiful children. I knew they had been safely tucked in by their favorite babysitter, but I needed to kiss them again and again, goodnight. I bowed my head, closed my eyes and thanked God for the treasure of their lives.

That was the darkest night of my life, and yet I know I was supposed to be there. I will never forget Joshua lying motionless on the road, wrapped in his favorite college football letter jacket. I will never forget his face or his name. I will never forget the terror I saw on the faces of the parents and the woman driver. Most of all I will never forget the impact this special boy continues to have on my life.

Yes, it seems Joshua passed away far too young. Now I also realize, as painful and traumatic as the experience was, I had the privilege of sharing in the last few moments of a lovely child's life.

His loss reminds me to be thankful for each day, for we do not what tomorrow brings. Because of Joshua, I am reminded to love more deeply, to share with friends and family life's special moments and to never hesitate to reach out to someone in need.

By now, Joshua would have been close to twenty-five years old. As unlikely as it may sound, I'd like to think he suits up each afternoon to play the role of quarterback for his championship team, "The Heavenly Angels."

"No act of kindness, no matter how small is ever wasted."
—Aesop, ancient Greek storyteller

"No one is useless in this world who lightens the burdens of another."
—Charles Dickens, author

"You can't live a perfect day without doing something for someone who will never be able to repay you."
—John Wooden, basketball player, coach, author

A life lesson in... asking what would Jesus do?

It's been almost twenty years since I laid my eyes on what I thought must be an animal lying in the middle of a dark, yet familiar road. On that unimaginable evening the Lord knew I would be passing by on my way to an event for my youngest child, my only son. He knew my love for children and people in general. He also knew there were times people didn't understand how deeply my heart ached for the needs of others. Frankly, sometimes I don't understand either. But that night nothing else seemed to matter, except for the precious young boy lying unconscious in the middle of the dimly lit road. Without thinking twice, I ran to his side having no idea what I'd find before me. "What would Jesus Do?" I thought. My insides shook ferociously, my heart raced like a thundering herd but in the midst of that horrifying experience, God gave me an unexplainable comfort so that I might do the same. He bore my intense fear and anxiety so that I could sit with Joshua until help arrived. I will never forget that night. Nor will I ever forget the feeling of helplessness. I will never forget God's hand upon me in a situation every parent sees as their worst nightmare. God literally held me in His loving arms and I held Joshua in mine as he went to be with the Lord.

Dear Lord, thank You for giving us strength when life seems impossible. Thank You for Your awesome power and love in the midst of trying times. Dear Lord, remind us to ask, what would You do---because You make even the darkest nights, bearable.

Amen

14

The Stranger

> "Be not forgetful to entertain a stranger,
> for thereby some have entertained angels."
> Hebrews 13:2

Summer vacation was nearing the end. My three children and I were planning a glorious five-day vacation in the Bahamas. Our destination: The Ocean Club in Nassau. My husband suggested I take the kids down for a few days until he could break away from his hectic office schedule to meet us.

It seemed everything in life revolved around his agenda, and by the time one deal was sealed, another seemed to be imminent. For this reason, our island getaway turned out to be more of an escape than a true vacation. We'd just moved into a beautiful Mediterranean home on the Intracoastal Waterway with bathrooms I literally never used! The house was quite large, and the kids and I weren't terribly excited about our new sprawling abode.

We loved our former house. It sat nestled on a creek with children their own age and friends I really cared about. If one child in the neighborhood got hurt, a neighbor was close by to lend a helping hand. Each day a gaggle of mothers waited for their children to return home from school. This cul-de-sac crew caught up on the news of the day while the children paddled off on a nautical adventure in a neighborhood canoe, but after several lengthy discussions, my husband made the decision to sell our much-loved home. He insisted we needed a larger house for the sake of his new business. I left this in God's hands for He knew exactly what we needed and why. I didn't need to ask—I simply needed to trust Him.

On this trip I had no idea what to expect from our Bahamian getaway, but I was ready for a change, a break from reality. Our itinerary had been faxed to the house by my husband's assistant, our tickets were waiting at the airport, and we had enough baggage to last at least one month. The Chalks seaplane, although a bit noisy, took off from Miami International right on schedule.

We arrived in Nassau just after lunchtime, leaving plenty of time to explore the outdoor market. The kids experienced bargaining at its finest. They had never been in a store where prices were negotiable! After several hours, completely exhausted, we dragged ourselves back to the hotel, threw on our bathing suits and headed to the beach, where it was truly a beautiful day on Paradise Island.

I found a couple of vacant lounge chairs and plopped down with a magazine and my devotionals, watching my three little fish frolic along the shore. For the first time in years, we left our sometimes frantic, usually dysfunctional way of life behind. *Thank you Lord for this magnificent retreat from everyday life,* I prayed.

An elderly gentleman sitting close by smiled as he watched my kids jumping and splashing in the sparkling waters of the Atlantic. He sat alone, a pipe clenched gently between his teeth and the look of a bittersweet memory on his weathered face. On the days that followed, we began to refer to the unknown man who watched us closely at the beach as "The

Stranger." The man was a stranger to us, but not to Jesus. Jesus knew this man and why he was there.

I didn't think too much about it until the fourth day. After a warm afternoon on the shore, we all needed a nap. I motioned to the kids and pointed to the poolside shower. As I started toward the steps The Stranger stretched out his hand toward me and cleared his throat. "Excuse me madam," he said.

A bit curious, I hesitated and replied, "Oh, hello." I told my oldest daughter Lizzy to take the younger two up to the room and I would join them.

"This will only take a minute or two," he said.

Much to my surprise he began, "I've watched you and your children every day this week, you may have noticed."

I nodded, yes, feeling slightly uneasy. "I have never seen such love and respect between a parent and her children," he continued. "About a year ago, I lost both my wife to cancer and my only son in a terrible accident."

I felt a lump in my throat and my lower lip began to quiver. "You and your children have given me back the memories and the hope I thought I'd lost . . . and I wanted to thank you." Then, he provided the real clincher. "Your husband must be so proud."

Without even thinking, I shook my head and looked down. He obviously got the message. Fighting back the tears, I gently placed my hand on his shoulder and whispered, "God bless you, sir." Without knowing it, however, The Stranger's poignant words would allow me to begin to deal with the hurts and lack of self-esteem I had locked away for twenty years of marriage.

Selfishly I wanted more time with him. This lonely, gentle man had experienced a loss no one wants to endure once in a lifetime, and certainly not twice. There was nothing fair about it, but for a brief, unexpected moment, joy—unspeakable joy—filled my heart. Somehow I knew in my heart this unexpected meeting was meant to be. God was assuring me that He too had a watchful eye over this dear man and my own broken family.

My life and the lives of my children changed dramatically after meeting The Stranger. Exactly one month and eleven days after returning home from our island getaway, life as we knew it would be altered forever. On September 11, 2002, my husband and I separated, not for lack of trying... and trying.

Ironically, it was one year to the day after the tragedy of 9/11, which was also the day we moved into our newly built Mediterranean-style home. How well I remember that day too. The telephone man ran into the house and asked if a television had been installed yet. He had just received word from his dispatcher that a plane had hit the Twin Towers. In utter disbelief, I clasped the hands of my mother, my sitter Rosie, five very large moving men, and the telephone technician.

"Please, God, heal our country," I prayed, "and watch over the victims of this horrific tragedy. Please find a way to heal our family and fill our new home with love and peace." We all held hands as a second plane crashed into the Twin Towers and erupted into flames.

The tragedy that devastated my children and me is one that faces far too many families today. Yet, thanks to The Stranger, I know that in moments of complete and utter devastation God can bring us opportunities for new beginnings.

I hope one day to meet The Stranger again. Until then, I often close my eyes and smile, remembering the impact one man, a total stranger, had on my life.

As I look back I realize meeting The Stranger was an Appointed Moment scripted by my Heavenly Father. A wake up call. These moments of grace in the midst of life's trials are God's confirmation that He is watching over us and our pain is His pain, our joy is His joy. Yes, my life has changed since that day, more than I could ever have imagined, but today I'm moving beyond the devastation of divorce and I'm stronger and more aware. I will never forget The Stranger's face, nor will I forget his words that ultimately led me back to my true source of strength: experiencing God's Appointed Moments, my circle of special friends and hope for tomorrow.

> ## A life lesson in... Appointed Moments
> ## Divine Appointments
>
> Have you ever experienced an Appointed Moment? Dennis Rainey, president and CEO of Family Life, a subsidiary of Campus Crusade for Christ states, talks about this idea: "A divine appointment is a meeting with another person that has been specifically and unmistakably ordered by God. "He continues, "Yet I sometimes wonder how many of these supernaturally scheduled meetings I've missed because I didn't have my spiritual radar turned on." How often do we not have our spiritual radar turned on? What an honest and clear definition of these mysterious appointments predestined by our Father in Heaven, scheduled specifically by Him for our benefit. I've found these divine encounters or Appointed Moments, as I refer to them, tend to arise when we least expect them. This is God's way of telling His children, "I am in control if you will only watch and listen as I bless you through this moment and give you hope for another day."
>
> *Dear Lord, let us be watchful for the Appointed Moments You place in our lives to confirm Your Holy presence as we walk with You day by day. Thank You Lord for the "strangers" in our life that are messengers, ambassadors of goodwill from You. Thank You for Appointed Moments and unexpected detours that lead us closer to You and Your will for our lives.*
>
> *Amen*

"Let no one ever come to you without leaving better and happier."

—Mother Teresa, goodwill ambassador, missionary

15

David's First State Dinner

*"Show yourself in all respects to be a model of good works,
and in your teaching show integrity and dignity."*
Titus 2:7

One evening my husband called from his downtown office asking how long it would take to put together a fundraiser for the incumbent governor of the State of Florida. "About a month and a half, at the least," I said.

"Okay let's do it," he insisted. Click.

The phone went silent and my brain started overloading with to-do lists. My life ran on schedule for the most part due to my stringent set of lists I felt compelled to make on a daily basis. I couldn't live without them. "Listing," as I referred to this nearly involuntary act of regulating my day, made me feel better if nothing else, and usually it worked.

The following morning, after dropping Elizabeth, Caroline and Martin off at school, I headed to the local party rental business. Debbie, the manager and entertaining guru of the store, helped me decide on white skirted tablecloths for the seven tables, the fifty-six brushed-gold French-style dining chairs, and round glass fishbowls for each centerpiece. *One box checked off of my to-do list,* I thought.

That afternoon I told the children we would be hosting a party for our state's governor. They had already had the privilege of meeting him and his wife several times and were excited about the jokes "The Guv," as people affectionately called him, would be telling. Though the dinner didn't have a specific theme and children weren't normally seen at this type of event, I felt strongly that this should be a family-friendly event, with their presence bringing warmth and freshness to the evening.

"Let's run by the pet store," I said, thinking again about my list. "I need help picking out three goldfish to be part of a sample centerpiece." They went straight to the goldfish tank and picked out three sparkling ones. Later that night the girls placed a bowl on the kitchen counter and filled it with water. I put some red, white and blue crystals at the bottom with a small state flag of Florida centered in the middle. Carefully, they poured in the lively goldfish and then I secured white roses and dangling tree fern around the outside of the bowl.

"Girls, I present the centerpiece for The Guv's party," I said. "What do you think?"

"Everybody will love them," Caroline exclaimed. I certainly hoped so. Another decision accomplished. The listing system was working out quite nicely.

My biggest concern remained a caterer. I was considering four possibilities, three who had exceptional credentials and a vast knowledge of serving at notable functions throughout North Florida. But it seemed each caterer was far more concerned with pomp and circumstance and the ticket price than with providing an outstanding evening for the distinguished guests.

Then there was Turtle Market. With its casual beach-side setting, this small, enchanting gourmet shop was known for spectacular entrees and scrumptious desserts. Its head chef David wasn't entirely seasoned with this type of affair, but he'd helped me out on several less formal occasions, and his conscientious and humble manner were heart-warming. I had to choose between a highly regarded catering business with relatively low risk or follow my heart and use the underdog.

One day I wandered into Turtle Market to check it out again. I went past the mouth-watering Ahi Tuna and fluffy spinach potato cakes. Past the flourless chocolate cake, the sticky tart lemon bars and the key lime pie made with fresh limes from the owner's own tree. David greeted me in his tiny culinary man-cave and offered me a creaking stool. To his surprise, I explained the gubernatorial nominee would be joining fifty guests at our home for a sit-down fundraising dinner, and I wondered if he'd like to consider catering the event.

"Please don't feel compelled to give me an answer right away," I said. I wanted him to realize the significance of the event but didn't want to make him feel obligated. The next weeks would be filled with tastings and pairings, and I wanted to make sure he felt comfortable. A man of few words, David looked a bit startled at first. He asked if he should take a course in presentation or etiquette.

"You'll be just fine," I said. "You simply need to be yourself and prepare the culinary event of a lifetime."

"Is that it?" he inquired. "It would be such an honor to serve your guests, and I would make sure it would be an evening you'd never forget."

That was all I needed to hear. David clearly wanted to please, and would go to any lengths to make our guests comfortable. We decided to turn my over-sized three-car garage into a full-functioning kitchen. "I want the guests to enjoy the evening without any glitches or curious smells," he said, "with no chance of hearing a crash or bang in the preparation process."

We also decided on a seven-course dinner as a way to allow the popular governor to gracefully bow out at one table at the end of one course and proceed to another table for the next—a formal game of "musical chairs." That way every guest would have the chance to speak to him.

One little detail remained on my list: a visit from the Florida Department of Law Enforcement. My doorbell rang one afternoon, and a gentleman showed me his badge. He informed me SWAT officers would be placed at designated points during the event. An emergency phone would be set up in case of a state disaster. We went over the guest list, and he wandered through my house sizing it up for security. "Do you have any questions, ma'am?" he asked.

"Oh, no, it seems you have everything under control," I stammered. He said goodbye and I went back to my "normal" daily routine.

Before I knew it, the big evening arrived. The Guv and guests assembled, along with my husband, our three children and my parents. Instead of a stuffy stereotypical dinner, the event became a time to embrace others. My family heard him speak of his own family and the importance of building positive relationships within our families and within our communities. The passion in his voice and the look of sincerity on his face made me feel hopeful for our state.

Behind the scenes David had been working diligently. The menu consisted of red, white and blue salad, staged with prize-winning strawberries, fresh blueberries, blue cheese and a raspberry-vinaigrette dressing, to tie in the elegant symbolism of America. The entrée, plump tenderloin medallions, were laced with a brandy cream sauce, and freshly picked haricot-verts (green beans) and spinach-potato puffs. By the time The Guv had moved tables his seventh time, now for dessert, he was eating a special recipe the chef created with a family feeling: homespun vanilla bean ice cream floating atop a warm, fluffy cinnamon doughnut drizzled with melted caramel fudge.

David's First State Dinner

The hour-and-a-half fundraiser soon turned into a three-hour affair. Fortunately, the guests were not at all concerned with the SWAT officers hidden amidst the landscape around our home. Nor did the emergency phone ring in the den upstairs. David kept peeking into the dining areas to make sure all was running smoothly.

"I never expected to be serving the Governor of any state," David whispered to me at the end of the evening. "But now that I have I will never forget your giving me the chance." He continued humbly, "I hope the Governor will remember this evening as a family event with good food, sincere conversation and hope for the future."

As the guests left we presented each with a Waterford Crystal elephant for their fundraising donations. I handed an extra gift box over to David.

"Oh no, this is too much," he insisted. "This is for your guests."

"Just because you didn't write a check for the fundraiser doesn't mean you weren't an integral part of the success of this evening," I said. "Your hard work and faithful resolve to stay out of the spotlight shows what kind of person you are. On this, your first 'state' dinner, please accept my sincere thanks. You made tonight memorable for so many people."

We were still talking when The Guv walked over to say goodbye. "My plane," he said, "was supposed to leave an hour and a half ago, if that's any measure of what the evening meant to me and my staff."

These two men from very different backgrounds had more in common than they realized. One may have served as chief executive officer of the State of Florida, the other as a talented chef, but as they shook hands on that unforgettable evening, they shared a common bond: their faith in God and their dedication to serving others.

Just another evening, I thought, *in the life of a faithful chef and a humble public servant, with all the unexpected, unforeseen challenges. Challenges the Lord used for His glory.*

A life lesson in... unexpected challenges

There are not many times in life when we have the opportunity to entertain the governor of any state in our homes. At first, I thought, I can't do this. My husband and I had been separated for about one month. I never in my wildest dreams envisioned that could happen to me! I prayed for the Lord to give me His unfailing grace and fill me with great strength. And He did. More than I could ever have imagined. He did it for me and for His faithful servant David—willing to go far beyond his duties as a caterer to make the guests feel welcome and satisfied. Although that night was the beginning of a long and agonizing divorce, God showed me his faithfulness through it all. And for the guests who attended the fundraiser, what they remembered was exactly what I prayed for.... a dinner that would be enjoyable for everyone with a "family" theme that would be clear, despite our heartbreaking news. Even when life seems completely out-of-control the Lord steps in and says, "My child, you are precious to me and I will be there to catch you if you fall." He continues to do this over and over for me, and He will do the same for you.

Dear Lord God, You are our sufficiency no matter what our plight. You walk beside us in those times of sheer delight and unexpected challenges. Thank You for Your promise to never leave or forsake us. And thank You for placing people in our lives to remind us that we are not alone.

Amen

"Lives of great men all remind us we can make our lives sublime; and, departing, leave behind us, foot prints on the sands of time."

—Henry Wadsworth Longfellow, poet

"Obstacles are those frightful things you see when you take your eyes off your goal."

—Henry Ford, industrialist

16

Beverle's Boutique

"Rejoice in our sufferings, knowing that suffering produces endurance, and endurance produces character, and character produces hope . . ."
Romans 5: 3–4

In my previous life, my world revolved around my faith, my children, my friends . . . and my former husband's event schedule. My friends used to joke with me and say, "Have you seen the President this week or visited the governor's mansion lately?" Or "where is your next un-real destination?" They were having fun with me, but what they didn't realize was I had become a really good faker. This fairy-tale life was not the one I'd dreamed of.

The list of benefits this charmed life provided did not outweigh the deficits, at least not for me. The constant busyness, the endless rides on the social merry-go-round, the efforts to keep up with the Joneses and the lack of quality time with my children bothered me more than my friends understood. The grass is always greener, right?

With that said, one of the few benefits I actually enjoyed was shopping at Beverle's Boutique. I was instructed to "look", dress, and act the part of a politically-connected wife." The clothes were well-tailored with gorgeous fabrics and usually fit exquisitely.

The Jamaican owner of the boutique had no problem selling her unique clothing. Still, her self-confident personality sometimes tended to rub customers the wrong way. Naively, I thought if I could drown Beverle with kindness, so to speak, she would be transformed. What a silly thought! Remember I'd always been a fixer. So Beverle certainly would benefit from my friendly visits, right? The Lord had a different answer for my good intentions. He had two little words for me, "Let Me." Of course, I had to be reminded that the Creator of the Universe certainly knew what Beverle needed far more than I did. In fact, He knew Beverle as His child. He didn't need my help, just my obedience to His will.

One day I dropped in Beverle's after picking up my son Martin from middle school. The shopping center sat just a few short blocks from my house and Martin didn't seem to mind. Looking back, I should have called ahead to mention he would be joining me!

"What do you tink dis is a babysitting service around here?" she asked.

I cleared my throat and said, "Oh Beverle, I just picked my son up from school and needed to look for something really quick. I hope you don't mind."

Beverle stared at the two of us. "Well, let me git him a glass of water and see if he can sit hisself in de chair for a few minutes."

I had to laugh because my son was painfully shy and was not particularly curious for a typical ten-year-old boy. He would have been happy sitting in the chair doing homework or sipping his water for several minutes or more.

As usual, I found just what I needed in record time. My son barely moved an inch and Beverle appeared content. "Tank you, Mary Ann, for coming in," she said. "And oh, by de way, your son may stop by wit you anytime. He did not move an inch. I watch him very closely."

My son noted her somewhat forward personality, but I told him she was probably a little lonely. He shrugged his shoulders as we left.

The next time I visited, a young girl walked in wearing an outfit that Beverle didn't feel was up to the shop's standards. "Young lady," she remarked, "you might want to tink about shopping elsewhere. My clothes very expensive, and I wouldn't want to break your pocketbook."

The mortified teenager walked out without a word. I wanted to run after her. Beverle noticed the shock on my face as the girl turned away. I gently told Beverle how embarrassed and hurt the girl must have been, and I felt uncomfortable seeing anyone treated that way.

Beverle had known me for a long time, and she knew I had both her and the young girl's best interests at heart. "I was jest tryin' to tell de truth to her," Beverle said. "Mary Ann, you can't save de world all by yerself."

"I know Beverly, you're exactly right. The world could use *your* help too." She looked at me in complete shock.

If we choose to serve others, knowing that no one person is better than another, that no person is without fault, then our intent should be to serve with a servant's heart. In other words, we choose to treat others the way we would expect to be treated, expecting nothing in return.

A few weeks went by. I decided to drop by and simply say "hello." I wanted Beverle to know that no matter what, she would always be in my prayers. I realized that morning Beverle was hurting, really hurting. I just didn't know how much. I found her standing behind a glistening glass counter filled with unusual pieces of custom-made jewelry.

Before I could speak, she began, "Mary Ann, I haven't seen you in a while. I need you to say a prayer for me. My doctor tells me I have lung cancer, and I do not even smoke. Maybe it's about time to change my life."

Complete silence filled the usually lively boutique. "I am so sorry to hear your news," I said. "Please know you will be in my thoughts and prayers every day."

Over the next months, I watched Beverle's strong personality begin to soften. She reminded me to live life to the fullest every moment and to live each day as if it were my last. "We never know what direction life will lead us," she admitted, "or how numbered our days are goin' to be."

Soon when I stopped in to see her, it was no longer to shop. She no longer needed another customer; she needed a friend, someone to encourage her. One day she told me she wished she had more time to do things differently. I suppose I knew what she was trying to say.

Many of us live with a "regret list." Things we could have done differently to better ourselves and others. The letter we should have written. The kind word we were too busy to say. The apology our pride could not bear us to mention.

At the end, Beverle had changed—a sense of love, hope and generosity helped her embrace the true meaning of life. She reminded me how vulnerable we are under our well-kept exteriors. She declared the value of reaching out to others, even if the person appears unlovable. Indeed, we all need people in our lives that are willingly, time after time, to encourage us patiently to be the best we can be.

Beverle passed away not too long after her diagnosis. She had made peace with the world and with the Lord. Although she wanted more time, hope for her future in Heaven carried her through her last days on earth. Beverle smiled at the fact she had changed and she wanted people to know it. She gave me a sense of hope for others who were desperately searching for answers. The Lord reminded me that He is the God of answers, every day—even on the days we think He's not listening. Of course He is: for you, for me, for Beverle, for the whole world.

> ## A life lesson in... second chances
>
> Beverle figured out that it's never too late to find our Creator. She admitted, "It took dis terrible cancer to make me a better person." In her weakness, she accepted the truth of her illness and her past mistakes. She realized in the time she had left, she wanted to smile more, laugh more and get to know her God. I'm thankful that I got to know her and that she felt close enough to me to share her fears and her newfound faith.
>
> *Dear Lord, thank You that You are the Lord of second chances. You give us a choice and it's up to us to choose You. Thank You that when we accept You as our Savior, we are guaranteed Eternal Life.... forever.*
>
> *Amen*

Do all the good you can, by all the means you can, in all the places you can, at all the times you can, to all the people you can, as long as ever you can.
—John Wesley, Methodist Minister

"There is no exercise better for the heart than reaching down and lifting people up."
—John Holmes, poet

"Do all the good you can by all the means you can, in all the places you can at all the times you can to all the people you can as long as ever you can."
—John Wesley, Methodist minister

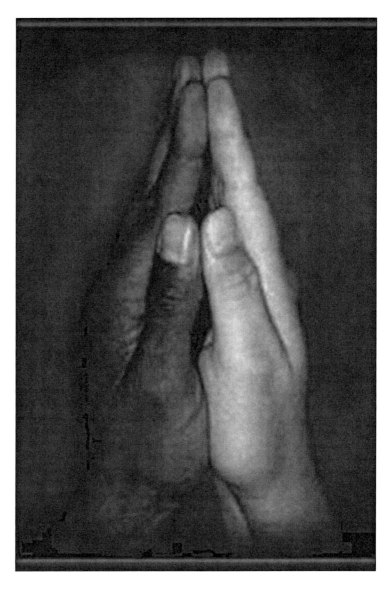

"Give thanks to the Lord, for He is good, His love endures forever."
—Psalm 107:1

17

Reggie's Grateful Heart

"But the fruit of the spirit is love, joy, peace, patience, kindness, goodness, faithfulness, gentleness, self-control; against such things there is no law."
Galatians 5:22–23

Several years ago, my kids and I moved for the seventh time within eight years. Thankfully after seven tries we found the perfect arrangement for all of us. We were looking for a place that felt like home—a place where we felt God was leading us. We finally found it, thanks to much prayer and an amazing realtor named Jayne. Because the moving company I had used in the past was unavailable, I phoned my friend Wade and asked if he knew anyone who needed to make some extra money.

"I've got just the man you need," he exclaimed. "Reg has worked for my family for many years doing odd jobs and just about anything you can think of. He's trustworthy and a hard worker."

"But there is something you should know," Wade confided. "Reggie can be a bit clumsy, and he has a slightly nervous personality. Still, he is loyal and committed to the people he works for, and he needs the money."

Reg and I agreed to meet at a bus stop a few minutes from my house. I drove up not knowing what to expect. A tall, slender, black man, grasping several boxes of hamburgers in his hand, walked out of Krystal Burger near the bus stop.

"Excuse me sir," I said. "Are you by any chance Reggie Wilson?"

The gentleman answered, "That would be me. It's a pleasure. What we got goin' on?"

I explained we had about three days to move into our new house and quite a bit of packing to do.

"No problem, no problem, we'll git it done, sugar." Reggie's high-pitched southern twang was contagious, along with his smile.

As we drove toward my new house, Reg talked about his wife Muriel, a retired school bus driver who was twenty years his senior. "She doesn't look a day over forty, but Lord only knows she's closin' in on seventy. She gets a little feisty every once in a while but God knows I love her. Muriel is like a little piece of heaven with a drop of spice." He told me she had recently been diagnosed with cancer but treatments seemed to be going well.

"I'll be praying for Muriel," I said.

"Oh, thanks, darlin'," he replied. "You are a gem."

I couldn't help but smile. "Reggie, you're a breath of fresh air."

"I 'preciate you gettin' me out from the 'hood and helpin' me out. I just love bein' down at the beach, and all my friends get a little jealous when I tell them I'm jumpin' the bus to see my folks on the other side of the tracks."

He smiled and covered his mouth, but out popped a joyous, "Oooeee."

As we pulled into our neighborhood, Reggie's eyes opened wide and he rubbed them in amazement. "Now I know why I love leavin' the 'hood.

I can enjoy someone else's home and then go home and wait until I get out of the 'hood again. It's all good, it's all good."

I didn't know whether to laugh or cry. This honest, charming man had touched my heart and reminded me that, in spite of my current circumstances, I had been blessed.

At the house, I gave Reg some final instructions and, quite frankly, I felt as if I had known him all my life. "I got this Mary Ann," he said. "This ain't no problem," and he thanked me for giving him a chance.

"That's what life is all about isn't it Reg?" I asked.

"Sure enough, it is. We're walkin' down a lonesome road if we can't help somebody who needs it," Reg replied.

"You're exactly right," I said. "I hope I can always remember that."

Now after about eleven years and eight moves, including kids going to college, moving in and out of apartments, and ordinary handyman jobs at my house, this skinny, gangly and slightly nervous man has become a part of our family. When he was down on his luck, I paid his electric bill, or put a small deposit in his checking account. From time to time I called just to say hello, and he did the same.

At one point Reggie ended up losing his car and had to move out of his house. Soon after, my parents surprised my daughter with a new car and all of us agreed Reggie should be the recipient of the "Old Red Blazer." I called him one afternoon to tell him the news and he stuttered for a moment.

"Lordy, I just can't even talk right now child," he whispered. "Can you give me a little while to just take all this in? I am so grateful. I just don't want you to hear a skinny old black man cry. It's not a pretty sound, believe me."

Many months have passed since that last move, and he continues to call and tell me to take care of myself because he just can't live without me. I feel the same way. Two people from completely different sides of the tracks can not only be friends, but share moments that otherwise might have escaped us.

He jokes around and says, "You know some people in your classy neighborhood might be wonderin' what's going on between a skinny white girl and an even skinnier black boy."

I say, "Very funny, Reg. You know you're like the big brother I never had.

"I know, I know," he responds, "and I'm grateful for that darlin.'"

Ever since my friend Wade recommended the slightly nervous and forgetful handyman, ever since my first encounter with Reggie at the Krystal Burger parking lot, I've seen the beauty of how believing in someone can change that person's life—and yours, too! Through the years, Reg and I have shared moments of laughter, prayer, love, tears and hard work. Accordingly, my trusted employee has become my faithful and loyal friend. Every morning, like clockwork, I receive a wake up text message from Reg. "Mornin' Sunshine, have a good day," he declares. It makes my day.

I'll always remember one of the first pieces of his modest wisdom he shared with me, "We're walkin' down a lonesome road if we can't help somebody who needs it." He was exactly right.

"What the world needs is a new kind of army—the army of the kind."
—Cleveland Amory, author, reporter, commentator

"When you dig another out of their troubles, you find a place to bring your own."
—author unknown

A life lesson in... old-fashioned wisdom

My friend Reggie has taught me so much about living each day as if it were your last. He's shared stories of being a young, very young father not knowing where to turn but he says, "I might not have knowed it at the time but now I know Jesus was wit me all the way, every day. You just got to talk to him." And he was right. God's love kept Reg going and that same love brought us together as friends. Reggie raised three successful boys as a teenager, and their love for one another and their father is remarkable. Drawing on his home-spun wisdom, Reggie says, "the only way to get through this life is to talk to Jesus every day and to help all the people you can because you never know when the bell's gonna ring and it's time to go home."

Dear God, Let us all be ready when the bell rings and it's time for us to join You in our eternal home. While we are on this earth let us choose to do Your work: to be patient, kind, and show mercy to those who need a little extra encouragement. Grant us peace, dear Lord, and let that peace flow from our hearts into the hearts of others.

Amen

18

A Packed House for Muriel

"To everything there is a season, and a time for every purpose under the heavens: a time to be born, a time to die; a time to plant and a time to pull up what is planted . . . a time to mourn and a time to dance."
Ecclesiastes 3:1 2–4

One March morning, I received an earlier than usual call from my handyman and loyal friend, Reggie. For the most part, he checked in by text, not a phone call and definitely not so early in the morning. He knew I left my house around 7:30 A.M. to take the kids to school and normally he waited until sometime after 9 A.M. to text me. *What's going on with Reggie,* I wondered.

"Everything okay Reg?" I asked hesitantly.

There was mostly silence and a slight sigh on the other end of the line. "Mary Ann, I just had to call you. She's gone. Muriel's gone, and I don't know when I'll be able to breathe again."

At that moment I had no true words of wisdom except to say, "Reg, your partner in life loved you so and now she's in Heaven, again waiting for you."

Reggie was known for running late and most people just accepted it, everyone except for Muriel. Even though she had been retired for years, she was used to being prompt. Her longtime job as a school bus driver required punctuality five days a week. Reggie had spoken honestly about his relationship with his lifelong partner. She would call sometimes when he was working to see if he was really where he said he would be. She ran a tight ship! He would laugh softly under his breath with his hand over his mouth.

I took a deep breath after his initial news and just waited for him to say something, anything. He hesitated again for a moment, and cleared his throat. "Hold on just a second, Mary Ann, I'll be right wit ya. Lemme just get a hold of myself for a minute." There was a brief silence and he stammered, "I guess you're right," he said. "She was always waitin' on me, and I guess she's still waitin', and I'll be there with her someday."

"Oh Mary Ann, now I have hope. Now I'm sure I'll be up there with the good Lord and my girl Muriel."

Reggie went on to tell me he was going to be strong and keep really busy and that would help him. He then continued, "Now I want you and Wade at the service next Saturday. I can't do this without my white sister and white brother."

My friend Wade and his family had known Reggie for many years. After all, I had Wade to thank for introducing me to him years earlier. "We'll be there, don't you worry," I told him.

The day before the funeral Reggie called to give me directions to the church and instructions on where to park. "When ya'll git there you just park around back, and I'll make sure your car's safe."

That statement made me a little hesitant, but I wouldn't miss Muriel's service under any circumstances.

Wade and I drove to the north side of town, arriving at the A.B. Coleman Mortuary right on time. Family and friends were gathering in the parking lot. We hugged, shook hands, met the nearest of kin, and listened to stories of happiness and joyful moments, all part of a dear one passing on. Wade and I felt like we were being honored and accepted into the family before we even entered the church that day. "Ya'll is just like my family, ya hear," Reggie said walking toward us. "God bless ya'll for makin' it. I'm just a little nervous and ya'll makin' it feels just right. It's gonna be all right now." The parking lot was packed. The last minute guests were filing in. "We best be gittin' to our seats," Reggie said. "Let's get this thing started." That was Reg, always ready for the task at hand and a little anxious on the way to wherever he was going. It was certainly no different this day.

Every seat in the tiny church was filled. It was a good lesson in humanity at its most final hour. The issue of race, religion, social background or political affiliation had no bearing on the events of this particular day. We all had gathered to celebrate the life of this strong-willed and beloved woman.

Among the people celebrating Muriel's life was a handsome twenty-something-year-old man, who confidently walked up to the pulpit. He was Muriel and Reggie's grandson, Jonathan Williams, who was studying to be a minister. He placed his hands on the pulpit, leaned back and greeted the audience.

"Hello, how are you all doin' today?" he opened.

Kind of a strange question to ask on a day such as this, but he continued. "I said, hey y'all, how are you doin' with those sad faces out there?" He cleared his throat for a moment. "I believe ya'll need some hope today."

The church remained completely silent. Not a single word, not an involuntary cough, not even a whimper could be heard from the mourners.

"Does anybody know what time it is?" he insisted. People began looking down at their watches.

"Okay," he said. "Does anybody in this audience know what time it is?"

Still utter silence. "It's God's time. Every moment in life or death, it's God's time. When we get up in the mornin' and when we go to bed at night, when we feel happy or sad, when we don't know what to say, it's always God's time."

Jonathan continued, "Muriel lived a long and successful life with many memories of her children, her family and her friends. She was a fighter. But when she closed her eyes for the very last time, God had already decided He needed another angel. . . . Remember, it's always God's time."

Jonathan's words opened my eyes to the wonderful reminder that we're continually cradled in God's loving hands. I was reminded that He will never leave us or forsake us. His timing is flawless.

As we prepared to leave the uplifting ceremony, one of Muriel and Reggie's friends aptly said, "We're so glad ya'll were able to hang with us today." He continued, "We're all people just tryin' to make it in this big ol' world." The insightful gentleman was exactly right. We're all at different places in our journey, but each of us must make a decision to stay where we are or reach higher and deeper to find the answers before God calls our name—for the very last time.

Most importantly, with Jonathan's convincing reminder still echoing in our ears, I thought, *we should do our best each day to make a small difference. Life is short, sometimes far too short, it seems, so live every moment of every day in God's time. Hope in Him and He will do the rest!*

> ## A life lesson in... God's perfect timing
>
> Jonathan Williams, a young man following God's call for his life, still working toward his degree, stood front and center at the tiny chapel at A.B. Coleman Mortuary, giving the audience the sermon of his lifetime. His faith and love for his family was evident... and he was not ashamed of the gospel of Jesus Christ. In fact, he had a few squirmers in their seats wondering how a young man had such a mature knowledge of God's word. Although young, he was wise beyond his years—obviously a gift from the Lord. I'll never forget those first commanding words, "Hey ya'll with those sad looking faces, does anyone know what time it is?" He knew exactly what time it was and he was excited about it. "It's God's Time," he shouted. And he was exactly right.
>
> *Thank You God that every day is Your time—Your perfect will is being perfected in us every morning we open our eyes. Let us remember this and put our hope in You and Your will for all of our lives. Remind us who You are and who You will always be: Wonderful, Counselor, Mighty God, Prince of Peace. We praise You, the Great I am.*
>
> *Amen*

"Perhaps they are not stars, but rather openings in heaven where the love of our lost loved ones pours through and shines down upon us to let us know they are happy."

—Inuit saying

"Jesus answered Him, 'what I am doing you do not understand now, but afterward you will understand.'"

—John 13:7

19

A Time for Amy to Breathe

"But they who wait for the Lord shall renew their strength; they shall mount up with wings like eagles; they shall run and not be weary, they shall walk and not grow faint."

Isaiah 40:31

In reflecting over the various events and memorable periods in my life, I have come to appreciate the simple, unremarkable small things.

From a simple visit with a complete stranger at the local grocery store to quiet conversations at the homeless shelter, I continue to give thanks for the small things, a chance for me to feel more connected to the people in my community. I remember family and friends asking me why I felt so strongly about helping others. There were times I asked myself the same question. Then I remembered my parent's example and their charge to be grateful for what we had and to use our resources to help those in need not because we always felt like it but because God called us to do so. No matter what people thought of me I had to ask myself, "Why bother?" The answer is, quite simply, "Why not?" These small, simple things lifted my soul.

One afternoon my oldest daughter Elizabeth had experienced a tough day with her seizure disorder. I didn't want to leave her alone, but my son needed to be picked up at school. Her sister Caroline offered to sit with her until I returned. After picking him up I called and learned Elizabeth was feeling better and resting comfortably, so Martin and I decided to grab a quick bite to eat.

We walked into Sonny's, his favorite barbecue restaurant, sat down and mentioned to our server, Amy that we didn't have much time. Then noticing she didn't seem like her usual bubbly self, I asked, "How are you? Is everything okay?"

"Oh, I'll be all right," she said. "Thanks for asking."

My son gave me a funny look like, *Mom, we're in a hurry. We really need to eat. What are you going to do?*

"I just want to make sure Amy is all right," I told him.

After four years of eating lunch at Sonny's almost every Wednesday I had gotten to know the servers fairly well. Amy now sat at the far end of the restaurant with a young man I had never seen before. She held her hands over her face, and the man who I assumed must be her son didn't look much happier. They talked throughout our meal, something Amy never had done before. She was always on the go, getting to as many tables as she could in her friendly manner.

I asked my son to give me a minute. I was going to wash my hands and check on her. He rolled his eyes and said, "Okay Mom, but . . ."

"I know honey," I said. "We need to go."

When I exited the restroom, Amy got up to bring over the check. I met her in the back of the restaurant and asked if I could do anything. "Oh, really I'm fine," she said. "It's just my son."

From what I could gather he was having trouble with his car and he couldn't get to work. Earlier in the week I had balanced my checkbook.

I am a fanatic about that, and miraculously I had made a mistake in my favor—an uncommon occurrence for me! I had no idea how much cash I actually had in my wallet, but I closed my eyes and said a silent prayer for Amy and her son. They were obviously having a rough time. I unzipped my wallet and Amy backed away.

"Please take this. I made an unusual mistake in my checkbook and now I know why."

I'm still not exactly sure how much money was stuffed in my wallet that day, and I don't think I was supposed to know. Tears ran down Amy's face and she gave me a hug. "Thank you so much," she exclaimed. "I never expected this to happen to me."

"Me either," I said.

I thought to myself, God has already written His script without our knowledge, and I'm so grateful He knows what we need, way before we do.

She hugged me goodbye, and I told her we would see her next Wednesday.

"Thank you again," she whispered.

"No, Amy, thank you for always being so kind to us and all of your customers. See you next week."

While I had talked to Amy, my son had finished his homework for the night. On the way home, we stopped off at the pharmacy to pick up some medicine for Elizabeth, who was sleeping. My son told me he would wait in the car.

"Mom, try not to run into any more people."

"Okay," I said, and gave him a wink.

Just as I turned to go into the store I saw an elderly couple struggling to bring out four extra-large cases of bottled water. I looked back at my son sitting in the car. He was shaking his slightly frustrated head! *I'm really in trouble now,* I thought, *but this will just take a second.*

Dressed in a stylish golfing outfit, the elderly woman barely made it to the car's trunk. Her husband, holding the second bundle of bottles dragged himself behind. "Oh, please let me help," I said.

"Oh, no," the gentleman insisted. Then jokingly he added, "Don't worry about my wife. She's a real workhorse."

I tried to hold back a laugh and said kiddingly, "You should be ashamed of yourself." "You're probably right, young lady," he replied. "I need a little reminding every once in a while. Who are you, the Thanksgiving Angel or something?" he asked with a gobble of sarcasm.

Together the gentleman and I delivered the last two cases of bottled water into the trunk. I waved goodbye and the couple rolled down their car window saying, "Thank you again."

Swiftly, I picked up my daughter's prescription and walked quickly back out to the car.

"Are you finished now for the day, Mom?" Martin pleaded.

"All finished," I assured him. "Let's get home to check on your sister."

All was quiet on the home front. My middle daughter proved to be an excellent nurse while we were away and my oldest was feeling much better.

I never wake up expecting to have a completely uneventful day—God wouldn't have it that way. I do expect the small Appointed Moments to fill my life with joy and gratitude for what I have been given: three beautiful children, a wonderful family, close friends and a collection of small things that make the big things seem much more bearable. These are gifts from the giver of all things great and small.

Small things keep us grounded and lead us into brief moments of Heavenly bliss with special people we may never meet again. A collection of small things when it comes to helping others can make the biggest difference, leaving hope for another day.

> ## A life lesson in... the small things
>
> Fifteen years ago, I might have thought, hmmm, small things: a new pair of shoes, a nice weekend trip with my children or a tasty dinner at a fine restaurant. Thankfully my view of "small things" has changed--drastically, I might add. The Lord, through the many Appointed Moments I've been blessed to receive has shown me the treasure in the small things in life; ladybugs, a migration of birds flying majestically across my lake, my seventeen-year-old Yorkie, and my amazing children who make my life a joyful symphony. It's the small things that make such an incredible difference for those whose hearts are open to them.
>
> *Lord Jesus, remind us of the small, simple things in life, like helping a stranger; lending an umbrella in an unexpected rainstorm (Florida is a great place for unexpected storms), or just being there to listen, the very thing YOU did while on earth. You are the Savior of the world and a Master Carpenter who knows exactly how to use the simple things to make people notice Your great majesty. Thank You for cool breezes, for breathtaking sunsets and even ladybugs!*
>
> *Amen*

"It is through the small things that we develop our moral imagination, so that we can understand the sufferings of others."

—Alexander McCall Smith, British writer

"Too often we underestimate the power of a touch, a smile, a kind word, or a listening ear, an honest compliment, or the smallest act of caring, all of which have the potential to turn a life around."

—Dr. Leo Buscaglia, author

20

A New Chapter for John D

"We have sent with them our brother, whom we have often tested and found diligent in many things, but now even more diligent because of his confidence in you."
2 Corinthians 8:22

Like my parents before me, I wanted young people to feel welcome and comfortable in our home. It was tucked away on a cul-de-sac where they could play football, basketball, and hide 'n' seek or run around back and jump in the pool, or even wade through the mud of the tidal creek which emptied into the Intracoastal Waterway. Putting on their boots, my son and his friends sloshed out to what they called Dolphin Island, pretending to be pirates. The girls frolicked in the pool, discussing their newest boyfriend or what they were going to wear to the upcoming school dance.

One of their friends seemed to hang out more than most of the others. My daughter Caroline had just started high school, and she had met a young teen I wasn't familiar with named John D. Usually we simply referred to him as John. Unlike John, most of their friends had known one another since they were youngsters. He was actually the first of many to call me "mom." His soft southern tone and sweet boyish face endeared him to me right away.

"Hey, Mom, how's it goin'?" he would say. He and Caroline, probably thirteen at the time, both had dirty blonde hair and small frames. They looked more like brother and sister. I called them my "little twins." They were the best of friends.

One night, several years later, I received a frantic phone call. "Hey, mom, it's me," he said. "I think I'm in big trouble."

I had never heard such desperation in John's voice. Usually he always had a smile on his face in spite of an often dysfunctional family life. "Are you okay?"

"I'm in jail," he said, "and I need your help."

I told him I would be right there. I called a friend for directions and then I phoned another friend, a retired attorney, who told me exactly what to do. I had no idea what a bail bondsman actually did, something I frankly didn't want to know. This was a lesson in life, with a capital "L," and I felt completely unprepared.

I drove up in front of a two-story, rundown stucco building in the middle of downtown Jacksonville. A tall, thin, and weathered middle-aged man greeted me at the screen door. I could barely eke out the words.

"You must be the one he calls 'Mom,'" said the bail bondsman.

"Oh, yes," I replied, "and I could use your help. I have no idea what is going on, and I am very worried about John. He is like my second son and, and..."

I felt helpless. I could only imagine how John was feeling. The bail bondsman obviously knew the ropes. This wasn't his first attempt to bail out a teenage boy.

"Well, ma'am," he stated, "just as soon as you write me a check for John's bail, I will make a phone call to the jail and we can start the process of having John released."

I was afraid to ask what the charge was, but obviously I needed to know. Evidently, John and some ill-chosen companions decided to take a ride in his brand new silver BMW and ended up in a not so desirable neighborhood. A police officer pulled them over, asked what they were doing and motioned for them to get out of the car. John had turned to one of his peers to see what was going on. "Don't worry about it," the young man said. John felt anxious and unprepared. "What's happening?" John asked. The police officer slowly shined his high-powered flashlight into the parked car. It didn't take long for him to search the backseat and pull up the floor-board carpet spotting a single bag of marijuana.

When John walked out of the jail's glass-paned double doors toward me, the look of despair on his face was almost more than I could bear. All I knew at that moment was I wanted to know the truth.

John talked so fast and faint I could barely understand anything. It seemed he was being framed for possession of an illegal substance, something he said he knew nothing about. He mentioned his new car was probably a red flag to the officers.

That night started a long process of lawyers, court dates, parole sessions and inquisitions by investigators. Along with John's current plight, he had a long history of a volatile family situation. His mother, a single mom and a special education art teacher, had lost most of her savings. Emotionally, she was drained. I offered to accompany John to his court dates and parole sessions so he might feel like he had an advocate, since his mother was having a rough time.

Throughout the next two years, I gained great insight into the young man I had previously known simply as my daughter's friend. His friendly, welcoming smile had faded into a tearful, hopeless countenance for a time. Every once in a while we would laugh about how simple and carefree our lives looked years before. In reality, we were both dealing with family issues that left us breathless at times, but John needed a mom, and I happened to have the privilege of standing in for the time being. Thankfully, his mother trusted me and knew I only wanted to help. There was no sense of jealousy or discontent. Quite the opposite. His mother readily admitted she had too much on her plate, and she appreciated John having someone he could count on.

After two long years of probation—paying his debt to society, a debt we later found out that he should never have had to pay—John began to heal. He enrolled in the local community college. He became a master computer technician and on many occasions helped out with my home computers, his way of saying thanks.

I often remember how my Uncle Frank, a professional at jumping hurdles and other trials in life, once told me, "Honey, I never really learned anything when I was on top of the world. It was only when I was in the valley that I learned the life-lessons God wanted me to learn. He taught me to fight for myself and my family. Those are the times that try men's souls, and those are the times faith and humility lead you back to a better place."

He reminded me that in the valley, is at times, a very important place to be. "That's where life-changing lessons are learned," my uncle insisted. John learned his share at a young age. Many of us deal with tragic and tumultuous circumstances. If we can step back from our own difficulties and show compassion and hope to another person, our lives begin to change, and instead of running into thorn bushes, we might be given the chance to run the race set before us and cross the finish line.

Despite his trials, John has been given the chance to run through a refreshing meadow toward a better way of life. He and his family are continuing to find their way. He called me recently to tell me he'd accepted the sought-after design job he'd been interviewing for after graduating from a school in South Florida. He graduated with honors.

As a young man, he has taught me so much; especially the importance of chasing your dreams no matter how long it takes! I've watched the transformation of my "adopted" son, ascending from a frightened sparrow, to the heights of a strong and wise eagle. I feel blessed to be a part of his life.

Although John D. is now traveling at home and abroad with his new job, he always takes time to call and say, "Hey Mom, what's up? Remember, I've got your back now." Sometimes we all need a "wingman," someone to look out for our backs and help show us the way, so we can jump through life's hurdles with strength and courage. We can be assured that Jesus is that wingman for each of us. If He is for us, who can be against us?

A life lesson in... having a wingman

John D. is one of those special young people who has been through times of complete brokenness and has risen to God's calling to persevere in the midst of strife, to never give up and to look back on his mistakes and be humble and grateful for his future. He is like a son to me. He always will be. Even still, when he calls me, "Mom," I get goosebumps. I'm so thankful for God's hand in connecting John's heart to mine, and for the privilege of being his second mom.

Thank You Lord for our children You have given to us for a short while. Let us be examples of Your love to them. May we surround them with hope for their future and teach them Your principles so they may one day teach their own.

Amen

"Angel marks allow a piece of your heart to touch the heart of a perfect stranger or your closest friend."

—M.A. Hammer

"See yourself always as a cause, and perhaps a better world will be found among your effects."

—Robert Brault, author

God reminds us in His Holy word that when two or more of us are gathered together He is in the midst of them. When we pray together in faith, the spirit of the Lord comes upon us and we are forever changed. It is a reminder of how blessed we are to know the Savior of the world.

"For God so loved the world that He gave His one and only Son, that whoever believes in Him shall not perish but have everlasting life."

—John 3:16

21

Oksana Searches for Answers

"And ye will know the truth, and the truth will set you free."
John 8:32

After using the same hairdresser for about thirteen years, I learned the owner of the upscale salon decided to retire after her longtime battle with cancer. I was pressed to find a new salon.

The first person I called for advice was my close friend, Karen. I thought, *who would know better than a self-described "professional hair salon inspector" who'd checked out most popular stylists within a thirty-mile radius?* She "shops" for hairdressers like most of us do for shoes or handbags.

"Are you familiar with the salon just off A1A in the Sandcastle shopping center?" I asked.

"Oh, I know the one you're talking about," she replied. "I went there one time and I decided it seemed a bit old-fashioned for me." Why do you ask?"

I explained to her about the untimely closing of my former salon and I needed to find a one. "I don't think you're going to like it there," she replied. "But go ahead, you'll probably like the people there; they're very nice." Karen sparked my curiosity, so I decided to make an appointment.

When I walked into the salon, a fair-skinned, dark-eyed woman stepped forward. "Oh hello, you must be Mary Ann. I'm Oksana. Nice to meet you. Please have seat, so I look at your face for one moment," she said in her strong, yet friendly, Russian accent.

I briefly explained the style I wanted, and she said in her thick accent, "No problem. I make you beautiful, a beauty, don't you vorry." Oksana's eyes sparkled as she prepared her work station. I could see that she took her job very seriously and wanted to make her customers feel special.

From our very first meeting her cheerful manner brought me joy. Within a couple of months, we began sharing our life stories, remarking on the similarities. We adored our children and wanted them to follow their dreams. We had a mutual admiration for people in general. We also were both dealing with broken relationships.

"Mary Ann, you are my friend. Vee understand one another, yes?" she asked.

"You are my friend Oksana," I replied.

"Oh, yes," she would say to the surrounding customers, "vee friends now and alvays alvays, Mary Ann, do not forget zat, ever."

On many occasions she remarked, "I love it ven people smile, don't you?" Despite her contagious smile and her admirable work ethic, Oksana spoke at times with a slight shakiness in her otherwise commanding voice.

We discussed her moving to another salon that might give her a larger client base and she mentioned starting English-speaking classes at the local community college. "I be good, Mary Ann. I goin' to learn better English and maybe move to New York City one day." Soon Oksana joined another small boutique salon. For a brief moment, I felt badly I had previously suggested she consider a move to a larger city to expand her horizons and broaden her talent. This was exactly where she belonged for the time being.

And yet, as we chatted, there was a still-small voice within me that made me question Oksana's happiness. It was the same insistent voice I heard throughout my life pushing me to conquer the skeletons I held onto.

Just a few short months after Oksana had transitioned into her new workplace, a storm brewed within her soul—a storm so fierce, it nearly claimed her life. The pain of her past life in Russia came to an unimaginable level of hopelessness. This beautiful and talented young woman tried to take her own life.

The salon called to tell me Oksana had been hospitalized and gave no further explanation. I feared the worst and I didn't even know why. Somehow, the connection between the two of us was deeper than I had realized. I sat and wept.

Four weeks passed and no sign of Oksana. I prayed for her and her daughter, and I asked God to watch over her. A few days later, Oksana's daughter called and told me what had transpired. She asked if I could try to help her mother.

What could I possibly do? I thought. But how could I possibly say no?

"Please have your mother call me," I told her. The phone went silent. Just after noon the following day, I received a text message asking if we could meet. It was Oksana.

"Anytime you're available." I texted back. "Please let me know."

We decided to get together on a Monday afternoon, the first of many meetings during her recovery. Her eyes welled up with tears as she told me of the pain she dealt with in her home country and the cruelties she had endured. She spoke of the undue discrimination against Christians and the guilt she felt for not knowing who God was. As an impressionable five or six-year-old, she'd watched Bibles being burned in front of her own eyes, and this had left deep scars with questions about life, love, and who God really was. She needed time to heal and find the answers she desperately wanted.

Several weeks passed as Oksana's will to live became stronger. She began to ask questions about God and His purpose for our lives. Her guilt, pain, and fear were all things I had dealt with in my past. Hour after hour we read the same Psalms that had once helped me; we recited John 3:16 together. "For God so loved the world that He gave His one and only Son, that whoever believes in Him shall not perish but have eternal life." (NIV) We read a variety of devotional books too, in hopes a word or a phrase would compel her to see the light.

One afternoon, after about three hours of these exercises in faith, hope and friendship, Oksana took my hand and asked me, "Vat are zee tings you fear zee most, my friend?"

My face went blank, as did my voice. *How could she possibly know I wasn't in complete control of my feelings?* I thought.

Oksana waited for my reply. I hesitated. "Oksana, I do not think of myself as a fearful person," I said, "but I realize fear controlled my life for a very long time. I realize I had allowed fear to literally paralyze a portion of my life for years."

The two of us then held hands, knelt beside my couch and asked God to heal our pain and calm the fear within us. In that heart-wrenching moment, Oksana bowed her head and asked the Lord to forgive her sins and make her whole. Tears of joy and relief poured down our faces. Not only had we become friends, we made a choice to trust Almighty God with the rest of our journey here on earth.

"Mary Ann, you make me happy and I vant to be good friend to everyone," Oksana stated boldly.

Oksana and I continue to be loyal friends, weathering the storms of life in a more self-aware and hopeful manner. Her newfound faith has given her courage. Her honesty has taught me to embrace the truth regardless of the price. Her kindness in the face of adversity has helped to renew my faith and my direction in life.

To my dismay, out of the blue, Oksana moved to another city where she would be happily reunited with her previously distant husband. My first thought was *what about my hair?* Then reality set in. I asked myself, what have I learned from this remarkable human being I have the privilege of calling my friend? She has inspired me to seek the truth, strengthen my faith, and follow my heart. God had placed Oksana in my life to remind me of His undeniable love, His forgiveness and His abundant promises. So although many miles may separate us now, the gift of shared faith and friendship remains constant and true.

"Jesus saith unto him, I am the way, the truth, and the life: no man cometh unto the Father, but by me."

—John 14:6

"Faith is to believe what you do not see; the reward of this faith is to see what you believe."

—St. Augustine, saint

A life lesson in... sharing our faith

Leading someone to the Lord is unlike any other joyful experience imaginable. I've been privileged to have three beautiful children and the feeling you have when that precious bundle is handed to you is hard to relay in words. Simply, it's a MIRACLE. I felt the same way the day Oksana and I knelt together in my quiet and cozy den as she asked Jesus to come into her life. My hands were shaking in utter joy and thankfulness. And she shook with emotion as she asked, "Dear Jesus, come into my life, dear Lord, I a sinner and I need You to make me whole person now." She continued, "Sank you vor zis day and vor saving my life." We both cried tears of joy and shared a bond that will forever connect us to one another.

Thank You Lord for giving us the opportunity to share Your saving grace with others. Thank You for the blessings You bestow on Your children. Bless those who share Your salvation message with others.

Amen

22

Deanna's Forty-Eight-Hour Plea

"Put on then, as God's chosen ones, holy and beloved, compassionate hearts, kindness, humility, meekness, and patience."

Colossians 3:12

My girlfriend was running a few minutes late for lunch. So instead of heading straight to the restaurant, I decided to drop into my friend India's store and pick up a cold drink. As I was waving goodbye, soda in hand, I said, "See you later, India," and that's about the last thing I remember.

The skinny heel of my sandal caught the corner of the mat at the front door, and I fell down on my right knee feeling like a running back slammed to the ground by a linebacker. I literally couldn't breathe and blacked out momentarily, scaring India to death. "What can I do fer you?" he exclaimed. "You hurt badly. Let me git you up." After several minutes sitting in pain, I felt a bit less traumatized and the concerned man helped me to my car. I'm still uncertain how I made it safely to the office of my physician, Dr. Budd.

Limping to the reception desk I was greeted by Deanna, the nurse I'd known for three years. "What have you done, Missy?" she asked. "You look awful."

Admittedly, I was pale and in pain but I wasn't dying, just slightly banged up. "Let's get you quickly into the examining room," she said. "You know, if you did a little less running around this type of thing might be less likely to happen."

Deanna had a way with words and she wasn't afraid to use them. Despite her straight-forward attitude, she had the heart of an angel, which could be seen as she attended to the diverse group of patients. Through the years, whether I visited the office for a mild illness or a full-blown colitis flare-up, Deanna stood waiting to share a comforting word. The more office visits I experienced, the more our patient-nurse relationship drifted toward a treasured friendship.

"Don't hesitate to call if you need anything," she would say. "Be sure you take care of yourself." Her motto was, "Life takes you down sometimes, but friends are there to pull you back up."

Due to the pain's intensity and profuse swelling, Dr. Budd did several x-rays. The initial ones were normal but he suggested an MRI to better view the bones and tissue surrounding the injured knee cap. He thought undergoing rehab for a couple of months would be all that would be necessary to alleviate the pain and restore my range of motion.

"I've got you set up for an MRI at the hospital for five o'clock," Deanna said, patting my back gently. "Now go home and ice that knee until your appointment."

I nodded my head. My daughters Elizabeth and Caroline had arrived to drive me home. The MRI that afternoon took about forty-five minutes. Then, the waiting game. I expected Deanna to call around lunchtime the following day to tell me the findings were all clear and to pick up my orders for physical therapy.

The phone rang earlier than I expected. "Hello, Mary Ann," declared a subdued voice. "This is Dr. Budd calling about your recent MRI report."

Why was the doctor calling me? I wondered. I was expecting Deanna.

Clearing his voice, Dr. Budd continued, "Would you be able to have someone drive you over to my office? I'd like to go over the MRI report so that we might discuss a treatment plan." Again, I was used to Deanna's cheerful tone calling me back about blood work results or to alert me a prescription had been called in for my colon disease or something even more benign than that, such as a sinus infection.

"I'll have my daughter Elizabeth drive me over as soon as you have an opening," I said.

"Now would be just fine," he replied.

I once read, "the dew of compassion is a tear." This simple, yet profound statement from the English poet, Lord Byron came to mind as my daughter and I arrived at the doctor's office. Deanna stood behind the reception desk with a crooked grin on her face, not her usual friendly smile. She walked us matter-of-factly to the first available room, took my vital signs, and asked how I was feeling. "He wouldn't let me call you," she suddenly blurted. "I wanted to call you first, but he said he should be the one to call." A tear rolled down her cheek.

I looked at Deanna not knowing what to say. Other than the annoying pain in my knee I felt fine. Why did this compassionate and devoted nurse look so forlorn? I wondered. Perhaps her fiancé who had been diagnosed with prostate cancer wasn't doing well, or perhaps her challenging financial situation had become worse. These were personal things I had learned about Deanna through the years and she knew I would be praying for her as she did for me.

"The doctor will be right in," said Deanna, hurrying toward the door. "I'll be just outside."

Elizabeth and I looked at one another in disbelief. This certainly wasn't the norm for Dr. Budd or Deanna. After knocking lightly on the door, the doctor entered and slowly opened my chart. He began softly, "Well, I have some good news and some bad news. Which would you like first?"

"Let's start with the good news."

He explained my leg would need several weeks of therapy to heal properly. "I think your knee will recover just fine over time," he stated. Grasping a several-page report, he then asked, "Are you ready for the bad news?"

Interestingly enough, I was. I had absolutely no idea what the results might be and yet I had an unexplainable sense of peace. Deanna walked back into the room just as Dr. Budd began to explain the findings of the radiologist who had studied the MRI. "There seems to be evidence of metastatic disease in several areas of your knee. We'll need to order a full body scan (PET scan) immediately at the hospital to determine if there is further growth throughout your body.

He was talking about . . . cancer. I looked over at my sweet daughter sitting in complete shock and then at Deanna standing with her hands clasped over her mouth.

"It's going to be fine," I said trying to comfort my support group. Deanna and Elizabeth helped me out to the reception area while the doctor finished writing my orders.

"Mom, no, this isn't happening," my sweet daughter whispered, fighting back tears. Not quite so reserved, Deanna began, "I'm already dealing with my fiancé and his prostate cancer. I need your prayers and your face to make me smile." Whether it was the last day of life as I knew it or the first day of the rest of my life, I knew Deanna had my best interests at heart because of the look in her eye and the tenderness in her words.

As I started to head toward my car I again felt her compassion and sensitivity. "You know, I've got your back—every day, any time, you just call," she said. She hugged me as her chest heaved with emotion. "I love you, Sunshine."

"Me too, you," I said.

No words could explain the deep empathy I felt from a woman who knew great trials herself. In the midst of her troubles she made a choice, a clear one, to embrace the needs of others every day.

The next morning, I prepared myself for a full body scan with a contrast die to show the suspected cancer's invasion of my body. Deanna called just before I left and said, "I've been pleading my case before God, asking Him to please keep you healthy and to perform a miracle." I thanked her for her kindness toward me and my family.

Driving to the hospital I began to realize the reality of what was happening and the love that surrounded me every day. Instead of feeling anxious, I felt blessed. The compassionate nurse who had become my close friend reminded me how precious life was and to be watchful for miracles. My family and I also prayed for a miracle and that God's will be done. Before going back for the PET scan we held hands and recited the Lord's Prayer. "Our Father which art in Heaven hallowed be thy name, Thy kingdom come, Thy will be done." My family and I felt complete peace. We headed home from the hospital, exhausted, yet hopeful.

Deanna called early the next morning to give me a full report. She said the doctor had given her permission to talk to me first. "There's just one thing I want to know before I share the results," she said. "What in the world were you thinking for the past forty-eight hours?"

The answer was so easy. "I can honestly say, no matter what you tell me, that I've been so fortunate to have such an amazing group of people by my side throughout my life," I said. I could hear a faint sigh on the other end of the phone. "The few things I would change pale in comparison to the many people who mean so much to me—people like you, my family and friends, and the faith which always seems to bring me through." I paused for a moment and there was complete silence.

"You really wouldn't have changed a thing?" she inquired.

"Okay," I replied. "Time, maybe just a little more time."

Deanna broke down in tears. "Honey, I told the doctor I had to call you today. We've gotten a miracle here. You are all clear. There's nothing there. We don't understand it but you don't have cancer and if you did, it's gone." We both cried tears of relief, joy, and thanksgiving. Our prayers had been answered.

For forty-eight hours, a compassionate woman pled my case before God while my life hung in complete and utter uncertainty. What a respected radiologist read on an MRI no longer appeared on a subsequent full body PET scan—unexplainable to all the well-trained physicians, but not to The Great Physician, who had other plans. His plans included teaching me to trust Him, even in the most distressing circumstances.

The Lord had graciously given the gift of time, and my close friend Deanna's prayers had been answered. Once again, the dedicated prayers of a friend offered me hope and joy for the future.

"Compassion asks us to go where it hurts, to enter into the places of pain, to share brokenness, fear, confusion, and anguish. It challenges us to cry out with those in misery, to mourn with those who are lonely to weep with those in tears. . . . Compassion means full immersion in the condition of being human."

—Henri J.M. Nouwen (1932–1995) Dutch-born Catholic priest and writer

"It's funny how, in this journey of life, even though we may begin at different times and places, our paths cross with others so that we may share our love, compassion, observations and hope. This is a design of God that I appreciate and cherish."

—Steve Maraboli, Motivational speaker and Author

A life lesson in... compassion

Deanna's story is ironic in a sense; it is the story of a woman who bears the burden of caring for an extremely ill husband. She works all day to come home to him, putting in hour upon hour to keep him somewhat comfortable. Her children endure financial difficulties, as does Deanna. But through it all, she's a servant to all who need her, patients and family alike. She deals with adversity on a daily basis and yet, the irony, she took time to pray for a patient who had become a friend—a forty-eight-hour vigil, when she too was at her wit's end. Her heart of compassion extends far beyond her circumstances.

Lord bless those, like Deanna, who live their lives with a heart of compassion, even in times of great adversity.

Amen

"He heals the brokenhearted and binds up their wounds."

—Psalms 147:3

23

A Circle of Friends for Bennett

"The Lord is near to the broken-hearted and saves the crushed in spirit."
Psalm 34:18

Since my children were young, I've enjoyed having their friends over to visit. It was a blessing to watch a diverse group of young people pass through our home. Often they would share their hopes and their dreams and sometimes even their mistakes. They knew I didn't mind listening—

the youngsters seemed to accept my urging them to be the best they could be.

"Okay guys," I would say to my children who poked fun at my soft heart. "You know how I feel about helping others and giving back to the community. I've always believed in encouraging others to strive for excellence."

"We know, Mom," they'd say. "You just can't save the whole world. Jesus did that. Don't you remember that's what you always tell us?"

They were exactly right, but that hasn't diminished my quest to touch others.

One afternoon my middle child Caroline brought home a new friend named Bennett. The

Young teen had been through some difficulties in his life. His decisions had not always been well thought out, but there was something about him that touched my heart. He was searching for a place to fit in—a place where he could hide from his teenage mistakes, the bad decisions, and the stresses of everyday life. A senior at Nease High School, he visited our home several times.

Later that spring, my son and I happened to be driving down A1A, the main highway, where a crowd of teens had gathered along a grassy area. No adults were in sight, and I wanted to make sure the teens were all right.

"You sit in the car for a minute and I will be right back," I said to Martin. He nodded his head. I walked over to the teenagers who were standing closely together in a state of shock. Panic was painted upon their faces.

"Can I do anything to help?" I asked. One of them tearfully repeated the heart-breaking story of what had just happened to their friend Bennett. The previous night the world he lived in came to an abrupt halt. The well-liked young man had pulled out onto the highway from a friend's house nearby where he had been visiting. In the dim light he didn't realize an oncoming car was not slowing down.

From the back of the crowd I heard a familiar voice. It was my daughter Caroline. "Mom, how did you know we were here?" she asked, pushing her way through the crowd. "I just heard the terrible news and wanted to be with everyone."

"I had no idea, honey," I said. "Your brother and I were driving by and we saw kids on the side of the road." Once again the Lord had placed me exactly where He wanted me, despite my own plans. Isn't that so like Him?

Tragically, Bennett lost his life, and a group of heart-broken teenagers lost a close friend. The group of high school students was not immune to heartbreak. Others too had passed away. Bennett was different, though. He had been an integral part of the close-knit group of friends.

"We are going to miss him," one young man said.

"It's not fair," another chimed in.

"What are we going to do without him? It's so sad," several others remarked.

I wanted to say something profound but nothing in particular came to mind. I knew they needed hope. They needed to know their friend was now in Heaven with no pain, no worries and all of his questions would be answered at last. I clasped the hand of my daughter and she in turn reached out to another and another. We formed a circle, one by one, bowing our heads in remembrance of their friend. "God, give Bennett's friends the peace that passes understanding." I stammered. "God, please show them your love and give them comfort and hope in their time of grief."

What do you say to a group of hurting teenagers whose lives had been turned upside down by the death of a friend? Not until a few weeks later did I figure out the answer.

Several of the same young people went one evening to a popular pizza restaurant to hang out and remember Bennett's life. Not so coincidentally, that same night I ran in to pick up a pizza for my hungry household, and some of the familiar teenagers walked up behind me.

"Hey, we just wanted to thank you for being there for us the other day," one of them said. "We were so scared and we didn't know what to do."

We hugged one another as a quiet confirmation of God's mercy began to grow within their hearts. These precious young people were learning how to grieve—and believe—at the same time. They were learning in times of grief to embrace hope and one another.

"You guys are doing great," I said. "I'll see you soon."

They waved goodbye. As I exited the local hangout, I realized how blessed I was to know these special young people and to share a small portion of their grief with them.

One of the greatest things I've learned throughout my journey is that what I have experienced has nothing to do with me, and everything to do with what I know are pre-arranged encounters, or Appointed Moments, brought about by the sovereignty of God. Of course, I couldn't save the world—that had already been accomplished by a humble carpenter over two thousand years ago—but we can all still help others through a tragedy. As Bennett's loss reminded me, sometimes all that's needed is simply showing up. The rest I've learned tends to take care of itself.

So what do you say to a group of hurting teenagers with wounded hearts? The answer: sometimes, very little. Just be there with a bushel of hope and prayers for their future.

"The emotion that can break your heart is sometimes the very one that heals it."

—Nicholas Sparks, author

"May the God of all hope fill you with all joy and peace in believing so that by the power of the Holy Spirit you may abound in hope."

—Romans 15:13

A life lesson in... hope for wounded hearts

When a young person, once so vibrant and full of life is taken from us, we all have questions. The biggest one, "Why?" And yet in our time of grief and sadness there is an answer that few of us think of at the time. The Giver of Life has His own timetable, completely opposite of ours. He has a way of showing us that He is in control—our job is to trust, even in the most traumatic of circumstances. He tells us in His word, "I will be with you even until the ends of the world." So, those on earth can be assured that our loved ones are not only at peace, but they are surrounded by the Peacemaker, The Father of Light. They have been taken into His Heavenly Throne room where no harm will ever come near them, ever again. And we will meet them when God calls our name. What a day that will be.

Thank You Father that You love us and our loved ones. Thank You that we can trust You when we are not prepared for their absence. Give us peace and joy knowing they are in Heaven waiting for our arrival. That will be a glorious day when we too, meet our Lord face to face.

Amen

24

Slow Down for Wheelchair Willy

> "For there will never cease to be poor in the land.
> Therefore I command you, you shall open wide your hand to your
> brother, to the needy and to the poor, in your land."
> Deuteronomy 15:11

My son Martin attended high school about thirty-five minutes from our home in Jacksonville, Florida. A few years earlier he had been diagnosed with a mild form of autism referred to as Asperger's Syndrome. Conversation was not his strong point, unless it had to do with college football or some other common interest.

I had carpool duty every day. Along our route to his school was the corner of Emerson Street and Spring Park Road, which was often busy, and made drivers and pedestrians cautious of their surroundings. Schools, barber shops, gas stations, the Children's Home Society, and a variety of other small working-class businesses brought a wide variety of people into the area. An all-night bar, called Wackos, sat on one corner.

Slow Down for Wheelchair Willy

After three years on the same route, we became familiar with Jimmy, the gas station attendant. We waved at the school crossing guard, and we saw the same children walking to school every day.

One morning traffic seemed unusually congested. Turning left toward Martin's high school, we saw that a man in a wheelchair was trying courageously to cross the traffic-filled side street. Martin took one look at me and said, "Mom, not today, please. I need to get to school."

I looked over at his handsome, stern countenance and smiled. This had been a "normal" form of communication for my son throughout the years. "Mart-man, this will take about two seconds." He somewhat respectfully rolled his eyes and smiled. He placed his hand forward, as if to say, *Go ahead, Mom.*

We looked at the disheveled man. He sat in his wheelchair with a lost look on his face. Traffic sped by and rain drizzled down. Forlorn and frustrated, he knew cars were traveling much too fast for him to safely cross the street. I made a sharp turn into the Wacko's parking lot—not exactly a place I intended to be that particular morning, or any other for that matter! The man kept his hands steadily on the worn wheels. "Excuse me sir," I called out. "It looks like you could use a little help." He never said a word. He simply nodded his head with a crooked smile. Slowly we pulled out into traffic and helped him navigate safely across the busy road.

The man placed one hand on his heart and with the other wiped tears away from his eyes, now sparkling. During the next several months I saw him a time or two. Each time I noticed him, he waved, and I felt my heart skip a beat.

Since my son has now graduated from high school, I came to realize I may never run into the solitary man maneuvering his wheelchair. There are days I wish I could ask him how he has been doing and how the wheelchair is holding up. I've gone back a few times to ask the nearby business owners if they've noticed Wheelchair Willy, as I call him. The answer is always, no. "We don't know him. He's probably moved on. Usually that's what these people do."

The truth is we were just two people trying to get by in this journey called life. We're often at the mercy of things beyond our control. The two of us happened to be privileged to share a few brief moments where mercy bound us together. His eyes told a story of their own and it was a blessing to see them light up!

A life lesson in... reaching out

Wheelchair Willy will always remind me of the blessings in my life. We never know from day to day where life might take us. Wheelchair Willy is obviously well aware of life's twists and turns. He smiled in the face of adversity as did our Lord, which in turn reminds me to be grateful in whatever circumstance I have been placed. For God knows our frame. He knows our needs. And He is in complete control, reaching out to His children, asking them to do the same.

Dear Lord, let us reach out in faith, providing mercy and hope for those in need, even when it might not be convenient, even when our actions are questioned by others. Let us listen to our hearts, let us listen to your call. Help us to reach out in love to those who are less fortunate than we are.

Amen.

You can never do a kindness too soon, because you never know how soon will be too late."

—Ralph Waldo Emerson, poet

"And we urge you, brothers, admonish the idle, encourage the faint-hearted, help the weak, be patient with them all."

—1 Thessalonians 5:14

The King will reply, 'Truly I tell you, whatever you did for one of the least of these brothers and sisters of mine, you did for me.'

—Matthew 25:40

A special drawing for me from one of my favorite little heroes—a beautiful young girl who fights cystic fibrosis every day with a smile on her face and a song in her heart and a dog named Sydney at her side.

25

Sophia and Grace:

A Grandmother's Gift

> But Jesus said, 'Let the children alone, and do not hinder them from coming to me; for the kingdom of heaven belongs to such as these.'
> Matthew 19:14

In life, you can read some people like a well-scripted novel. Others are a bit less transparent. Several years ago, my son and I moved into a new home situated on a creek with magnificent palm trees and oaks, twittering wildlife and a well-manicured golf course sitting just beyond Sawgrass Creek. Most of the residents were retired and enjoying golf at the nearby PGA course, while my son and I stayed busy trekking through life.

Once, as I pulled into my driveway, I saw Ann, my fiancé's mother sitting across the street wrapped in a blanket. Although she had just crossed the cul-de-sac she couldn't seem to remember how to find her way back. Another day she had accidentally locked herself out of the house and was sitting on the curb patiently waiting for my arrival. To add to all this busyness, my two daughters, now in their twenties, and their boyfriends would stop in frequently. Along with my fiancé's two sons and their girlfriends our friendly little cul-de-sac stayed quite active.

As I raced about I tried to remember to smile and wave out of respect for my new neighbors. Some of them waved back, some didn't. With Sophia, who lives right next door, it simply took a helping hand, offering to carry in her heavy groceries and we became new friends. One afternoon I spotted her standing outside her entryway with a handsome couple and a beautiful, young girl who looked slightly frail.

"I would like to introduce you to my daughter Nicole, her husband and my granddaughter Grace," said Sophia. When she introduced Grace I could see the sparkle and joy in a grandmother's eyes. There was no doubt about the deep love she felt for her beautiful granddaughter.

"Hello, how are you?" I asked.

"Just fine," replied Grace. "We have been at the beach today." Grace seemed tired and needed to go inside.

The next morning, I saw Grace peering over the balcony. "Can you come over?" she asked.

"I'll see," I said. "Let's ask Sophia."

It turned out Grace was in the middle of a breathing treatment and needed to rest afterwards. So I walked next door and found her curled up on the sofa. We visited a few minutes; she drew me a colorful picture of a tree, and I read her a story. There was something very special about the relationship Sophia shared with her lovely granddaughter. Sophia's eyes lit up as she watched Grace draw her picture. When her grandmother spoke, Grace obviously shared the same heartfelt feelings for her devoted "Ya-Ya."

"Our Grace has Cystic Fibrosis," said Sophia trying to hide the sadness in her voice. "You see, she must use this breathing machine several times a day to keep her lungs clear."

We chatted briefly, but I didn't want to wear out my welcome so I soon headed home. Closing the front door, I walked down my hallway to the den and turned on my laptop. This room, with its straw-colored walls and a large painting of Gerber daisies in deep, vibrant hues, was my oasis, the place I came for learning, reflecting, relaxing, and my hobby of practicing medicine without a license! Having two children with medical disorders, I knew the importance of learning everything possible about their conditions. For this reason, my friends and family jokingly called me Dr. Hammer.

I typed in "Cystic Fibrosis." I knew very little of the disease, but I knew enough to have a sinking feeling in my stomach. The average life expectancy of children with this degenerative disease, I learned, is anywhere from nine years to the mid-thirties. So the special relationship shared between Sophia and Grace's was all the more tender and heartfelt.

After visiting for a week or so I became very attached to sweet Grace. Her zest for life, her hopeful smile, and her quiet acceptance of her disease endeared her to me. I wanted more time with her, but Grace and her family had to fly back to their home in Maryland and prepare to move across the country to San Francisco. Knowing how difficult it is to care for an extremely ill child, I decided to drop a little something off at Sophia's front door before they took off.

My best friend had given me a hand-carved heart to signify our affection for one another and the memories that bound us together. Part of me didn't want to let it go. Another part of me knew precious Grace could hold it in the palm of her tiny hand when she felt scared or sick or had to go the hospital.

After dropping off the hand-crafted heart and a short notecard, I took a deep breath and whispered a silent, *"Thank you, God, for my wonderful children and please watch over Grace."*

From the day we first met, I've felt Sophia and I have shared many Appointed Moments, where we were meant to connect. Once in a while we'd fit in a quick lunch, which usually turned into a three-hour counseling session for both of us. We talked about everything from divorce and children to love, illness and forgiveness. Sophia shared her wisdom on going through trying times with her daughter and sweet Grace. I told her about my neurological episode which left me without a large portion of my memory. I confessed that Post Traumatic Stress Disorder had left me with nightmares, panic attacks and reliving some of the traumatic events of my past. I mentioned there were frightening moments of my life that I had never dealt with and without warning my brain went into shut-down mode. Not surprisingly, Sophia was one of the first people I had shared my memory loss with. Because of our sharing through the years, she seemed to understand more than most. She offered to go with me to doctor appointments and cognitive therapy (a way to help me deal with my memory loss) and suggested I take time to deal with hurts from my past. Sophia insisted that I needed to find my voice—a voice I lost many years ago.

Throughout my life, almost without fail, God has seemed to put me in situations that have provided me with exactly what I needed at the time. I believe these are moments of God's grace, and are available to all of us, perhaps more often than we realize. Yet many of us are not as receptive as we could be or should be. I became much more aware of these moments of grace during my road to recovery referring to them as "Appointed Moments." Moreover, the Lord continues to provide me countless, uplifting and grace-filled moments. One afternoon during my recovery... for instance, I rolled into my driveway to relax for a bit before meeting a friend for dinner. Much to my surprise a young, bright-eyed girl and her mother stood starring at my car. I didn't recognize them at first. I wondered if they were lost. Then, I heard the loveliest five words: "Mary Ann, it's me, Grace."

Although I'd forgotten my first meeting with this precious young lady and her Mom, due to my earlier memory loss, my heart knew better. I jumped out of my car shivering with excitement. "Grace," I hesitated. "Yes, it's me. I'm eleven now," she exclaimed. At that moment my loss of memory had no impact on the reunion with this special family or anything else. God had placed us in the exact spot He wanted us to be; together.

For the first time in many years, I cried and cried. Not because I was sad. No just the opposite. God was reminding me of His amazing love and grace using the gift of a grandmother's love and her delightful granddaughter named . . . Grace. All I could think about were the poignant words to the traditional hymn by John Newton (1725–1807) that we all recognize: "Amazing grace how sweet the sound that saved a wretch like me. . . . I once was lost but now am found was blind but now I see." Memories are fleeting as is life, but grace sustains us if we recognize the hand of The Giver.

Grace, God's grace, and the love of a grandmother who lived next door, had been standing at my doorstep all along.

"If, instead of a gem or even a flower, we could cast the gift of a loving thought into the heart of a friend, that would be giving as angels give."
—George MacDonald, Scottish author, poet and Christian minister

"Love that reaches up is adoration, love that reaches out is compassion, love that stoops is grace."
—Dr. Charles Swindoll, author, Christian speaker and pastor

A life lesson in... grace

Sophia has taught me so many lessons in wisdom and grace: "My dear, believe in yourself, do your best and God will do the rest." She reminds me to be still before making any major decisions, before stepping out into a new project. "Make sure you're doing these things for the right reasons and not because you think you have to do them or be someone you're not." There are times she has taken my face in her hands and said, "Just believe, my dear, just believe." She is absolutely right. She knows none of us is an island. We are all connected for a reason. God wants His children to live their lives for and with others, for without others we become frustrated and at worst, bitter. Let us choose to embrace grace.

Dear Lord, give us friends who love You and each other. Let us gain wisdom through our friends and Your word. Both are the true secrets to life and love. Thank You for the love of our parents, grandparents, children, and spouses. Thank You for special friends who encourage us to be the best we can be... even if we might not feel like it at the moment. Bless them all.

Amen

Love is the greatest thing in the world. My grandmother, Mary McKay Underhill celebrated love every day of her life. She taught us the importance of faith, love, never giving up and building strong family ties.

26

Mary, Queen of our Hearts

"She gets up while it is still night; she provides food for her family and portions for her female servants. She considers a field and buys it; out of her earnings she plants a vineyard. She sets about her work vigorously; her arms are strong for her tasks."
Proverbs 31:15–16

Sometimes the true measure of a life well-lived can best be assessed at its final moments on Earth. I was thinking about this as I looked out over the huge crowd assembled for a funeral at the historic St. Barnabas Church near Barberville, a small town of no more than ninety or so residents in Central Florida. The church was jam-packed. But I'm getting ahead of the story of how Mary McKay Underhill, my grandmother, wrapped her world for ninety-four years and eleven months in unconditional love.

Visiting her in Barberville during summer breaks, my two sisters and I were up at the crack of dawn, listening to the loud whistle of the Amtrak train that whisked along just behind her gracious home, and to rooster crows, and to her dogs—named Up and Down—barking for morning grub. With my grandfather confined to his lazy chair, Ganny, as we called her, was the unlikely person now running a large fern-farming business that provided ornamental greenery to floral wholesalers throughout the United States and Europe. She had her own special business practices, like early morning breakfast at the "Lil' General's" kitchen table.

Around 7 a.m., two of the fern foremen would knock on the back door. "Come on in, Red and Howard," she would call in her recognizable sweet drawl. "Get yourselves a cup of coffee."

"Oh thank you, Miss Mary," the men answered.

"Now girls," she'd say turning to us, "it's almost time to make ya'll some of Ganny's pancakes."

We would squeal for the fluffiest, most perfectly fashioned pancakes imaginable. The recipe was a secret, but we knew buttermilk was one of the key ingredients. "Don't get milk out, girls. Only buttermilk will work for Ganny's pancakes."

The antique iron griddle placed on the gas stovetop bubbled with a teaspoon of Crisco oil, the only brand she ever used. The more "fat" the merrier! She allowed us to take turns forming the batter into characters we called Buddy the Bear, or Billy the Bunny Rabbit.

Howard and Red would drink their coffee while Ganny made an impressive batch of pancakes. "Howard, you make sure everything's tended to just like Miss Mary likes it," the Lil' General would insist. "Don't ya'll forget to "pull weed" today." With weeds a constant nuisance in the fern business that was her way of urging her employees and family members to work hard and be dedicated to a job well-done.

"Miss Mary makes the best pancakes in the world, and this Joe ain't bad either," her long-time employees would state before heading out for a long, hot day's work.

Ganny would tell the men to have a good day, do their best and she'd see them bright and early the next morning. This was a daily ritual.

Then Howard and Red would head across the narrow highway to the packing house, a long narrow greenhouse-like structure with a tin roof that held the lush fern. A large group of employees would gather the leafy green bundles from the nearby acreage and truck it back to the packing house in the sweltering heat. (Eight of those early, loyal employees continue to work for the company today.) Under the umbrella of Underhill Ferneries, two new enterprises have been added—a wreath company, The Magnolia Company, along with a tree business, Seeds of Light—which is now run by two grandsons and one grandson-in-law. "We like keeping it all in the family," Ganny said later on. "It works so well that way at our house."

Everyone around her always felt loved. We would constantly hear, "Ganny loves you, darlin'" or "Ganny's so proud of you," in her slightly hoarse Southern voice. She was the mother of two devoted and warm-hearted children, Frank, and my own mother, Kay. Her kindness, her quiet faith, her almost childlike smile and the twinkle in her eye made us feel like we were visiting the queen. In fact, we girls started calling her "Mary, Queen of our Hearts."

Starting when I turned a year old, Ganny had sent a Valentine card every year with a dollar bill enclosed. As the family grew, so did the volume of thoughtful Valentines. Eventually she was sending thirty-six cards in February to her eight grandchildren and twenty-eight great-grandchildren, a thoughtful gift treasured by all. That was a lot of one dollar bills to send at ninety-something.

We knew her favorite book was The Greatest Thing in the World, written by a devout Christian, Englishman Henry Drummond. "*You will find as you look back upon your life that the moments when you have truly lived are the moments when you have done things in the spirit of love,*" writes

Drummond. I'd say Ganny understood these wise words as well as anyone I've ever known. She kept the thin paperback on her bedroom nightstand with her treasured family photos, her sacred address book and a fresh box of Kleenex tissues—always a necessity for a lady, she would say. All of the things she treasured, even a fresh box of Kleenex, were things she cherished in the spirit of the great love she had for life and her family.

We always enjoyed hearing Ganny tell us about growing up in Ocala, Florida, with her four sisters and her great-aunt who they stayed with after their mother died. They lived much like a scene out of Gone with the Wind. One night after Ganny and her sisters fell asleep, Auntie, as the girls called her, decided to take a short jaunt, without her trusted driver. Auntie was not used to driving during the day, so driving at night was an even bigger challenge.

Traveling down the dark dirt road, the genteel woman suddenly hit her brakes as the car brushed the front of an oncoming car. Auntie was handed a ticket, and the officer told her to appear in court. When called upon by the judge, a close family friend, as to the cause of the accident, Auntie asked, "Judge, how in the world can you charge me in an accident which happened after dark?" She then added, "And the driver was maneuverin' an impossible to see black car of all things."

One afternoon many, many years later, actually about three weeks before she passed away, I was visiting for the weekend, and Ganny called me back to her bedroom. She patted the side of her bed for me to sit beside her. "I must talk to you about something very important."

"Mary Ann," she began, "you are my precious namesake, and I need to know something. Have you finished the poem I asked you to write for my funeral?"

A bit shocked, I stammered. "Yes, ma'am, it's out in my car, tucked inside my Bible." She asked me to run get it. "Ganny needs to make sure I don't need to make any corrections while I'm still around," she insisted.

That was Ganny, the loving Lil' General. She was always in charge, always right on top of things, and always smiling. I raced out to my car and grabbed my lovingly worn Bible, delivering the poem to her bedside. She asked for her reading glasses and a sip of water.

"Let me see," she said as she tapped her finger across the pages. Slowly she began to read, "Mary, Queen of Our Hearts, we love you more than you'll ever know. Your laughter, your love, and your wisdom, have allowed each of us to grow."

When she finished, I asked nervously, "Okay, Ganny, what do you think?"

"Well, angel, I'll tell you what." Then her voice cracked faintly, and she regained her composure as usual. "Darlin', I have to tell you, I wouldn't change one little thing. I just had no idea I was that special."

Choking back the tears, I gave her a kiss, the last kiss of the millions I had the pleasure of giving and receiving throughout my lifetime.

Now at her funeral in old St. Barnabas Church, the pews were overflowing with at least 300 people. Before she had passed away, Ganny had told my Uncle Frank to please make sure the church was full—even if he had to pay people to come in off the street. She would have been pleased; no money had to be exchanged! Leaning over to my mother and turning his eyes toward Heaven, Uncle Frank whispered, "Well, Ganny, you packed the house out!"

Ganny had requested one other favor of her children. "Please give everyone who attends The Greatest Thing in the World," she'd said, so all attendees would receive a copy of this short commentary on love that had guided her long life. As the guests arrived, ushers were prompted to hand out a copy to each person in attendance.

As I approached the steps to the pulpit, the exquisite Tiffany stained glass windows showered the sanctuary with magnificent light. I slowly began speaking, "Today, we are here for one reason—to celebrate the life and the love of a woman I am proud to call my grandmother. But she was so much more than that. Her life has been an example of unconditional love to the many people she has met along her journey. I hope when we leave here today, we can agree to love, and strive to love all those who cross our path. Mary McKay Underhill believed that we should embrace one another, whatever the price, because love never fails, and above all, she was certain, no greater gift exists, than the gift of *love*."

"My angels," she would say, "never forget love is the greatest gift of all and that is what you will be remembered for."

Yes, in the final moments looking over her life, there was no doubt in any of our minds; our beloved Ganny was an angel from Heaven extending love here on Earth.

"Lord, grant that I might not so much seek to be loved as to love."
—Francis of Assisi, saint

"The true meaning of life is to plant trees, under whose shade you do not expect to sit."
—Nelson Henderson, poet

"My angels never forget love is the greatest gift of all and that is what you will be remembered for."
—Mary McKay Underhill, aka, Ganny

A life lesson in… Love: the greatest thing in the world

My grandmother, Ganny, had a quiet faith she held close to her heart. The sparkle in her eyes and the smile on her face in the midst of freezing temperatures and the lack of staff to load the packing house was in no way a hindrance; it was a challenge for God to show Himself strong. She was the Lil' General with a heart filled with love and consideration for all who knew her. As youngsters we'd hear people call her Miss Mary and the respect in their voices was as if they were talking to a queen. And in our eyes she was and will always be Mary, Queen of our Hearts, not because of what she did in her life, but because of the love she spread everywhere she went. She never gave up, she never gave in. She knew what was right, and she insisted on putting your best foot forward regardless of how you were feeling. She'd insist with her little finger pointing toward her adoring brood, "Always do your best, say your prayers, and be kind to everyone you meet because one day somebody will remember how much love poured out of your hearts, and that's the honest truth my darlin's."

Dear God, thank You for a grandparent's love—for their wisdom and great devotion to their families. Bless them Lord and remind us to be grateful for the gift of having them in our lives.

Amen

27

Dez's Unforgettable Smile

"The spirit of the Lord God is upon me, because the Lord has anointed me to bring good news to the afflicted; He has sent me to bind up the broken-hearted, to proclaim liberty to the captives..."
Isaiah 61:1

Dez San Agustin touched the hearts of those who knew him with his gleaming smile and his tender heart. There was nothing about this young man that was haughty or pretentious or self-absorbed. After all, at twenty-two, so many young adults are searching for answers or simply out to fulfill their own needs and desires. For Dez, life revolved around helping his family, working hard to better his future and most importantly, giving a portion of himself for the better good, expecting nothing in return.

The local Gate Petroleum food mart located on historic A1A, welcomed people from all walks of life. They catered to landscape architects, pest control engineers, carpool moms, wealthy CEOs, retirees, golf caddies and a handful of local sheriff's deputies, as if they were all family.

Dez's Unforgettable Smile

One warm sunny morning I pushed open the large glass-paned doors to pick up a cold drink. I said my usual morning hello to the store's friendly manager, Pat, who stood at the front check-out counter. I'd gotten to know this beautiful woman while running in and out of the store over an almost twenty-year period. She always asked about my children, she took time to listen and she too, always had a smile on her face. The commitment to her clients and her staff was obvious. As shoppers passed by she called them by their first name. "Hello, Susan," to a local gift boutique owner, "good morning." Not only was she the manager, she was a wonderful spokesperson for the company and a respected member of our close knit community.

Everyone knew Pat. She stood strong through her own share of hard knocks and she related to others in an insightful and caring way. She ran a tight ship, balancing the use of a firm hand and a heart of gold.

Dez was one of her special people. It was nearly impossible to miss his contagious smile. His thick dark hair, golden-brown skin and that smile, a smile that lit up the already bright and airy space, made a sunny day even more pleasurable. Dez had become like a son to Pat as had so many of her employees through the years. She called them her "kids." All of them. "But this one was special," she said. "He was my friend, my close friend. He took his job seriously and he liked getting to know the people who walked through our doors each day. He was humble, a hard worker and you couldn't overlook his smile. It made this place a happier environment to work in."

Pat explained that Dez came to a point in his young life where he wanted to expand his horizons. He didn't want to leave Gate completely but he wanted to move on in order to travel, meet new people and be a positive role model for others. "Saying goodbye to Dez was hard," Pat said. "But we cut a little deal." She laughed while explaining the deal. He would go work at Servpro in the disaster relief division while keeping a part-time position at the store. It worked well for everyone, and although Dez didn't know it, his continued presence was appreciated by the staff and customers alike.

The local sheriff's officers incorporated regular stops at the Gate Station for break time. At any given point in the day you'd see a deputy or two conversing with the employees and the townspeople. Dez even played golf on a regular basis with a few of the officers.

As the weeks went by, I started seeing less and less of Dez. That's when Pat mentioned he had taken a new job, which allowed him to travel and experience new opportunities that he was looking forward to. He still kept his roots grounded with the many people who cared about him at Gate.

"Good morning, Pat," I said, as I walked in one day. She looked as if she'd had a long night. Not her usual cheery self. "You doing okay?" I asked. A blank stare crossed her slightly ashen countenance. "It's Dez," she said. Immediately my insides felt shaky. Something wasn't right; the look on Pat's despairing face said it all. "Mary Ann, I'm sorry to tell you this, but Dez passed away last night." I gasped. "Pat, I'm so sorry." As I looked around the store, the staff and customers who frequented the family-operated chain seemed to be in shock.

Pat spoke as if she had lost a son, and, in a way, she had. Dez had become, like so many others, a part of the family unit at this one-stop shop. The same group of people walked in and out of the busy, local establishment on a regular basis. This was a place where they felt at home. Dez did too.

I remembered the first time I had met Dez several months earlier. He'd smiled, and wanted to know how my kids Caroline and Martin were doing. "You have to be Caroline's mother—you look just like her," he had stated. "And your son Martin always comes in to pick up a V-8." At the time I didn't think much about his remembrance of my children. Of course I thought they were extra special—so others must too! Not until I saw him interact with all of his customers in a similar manner did I realize he was uniquely special. He was determined to make customers feel at home—and they certainly did.

The last time I saw Dez he mentioned he and a friend would be leaving to provide relief to victims of a hurricane that hit Pensacola, Florida. He was so filled with love and hope for his future and those he had committed to help. Dez and his friend Adrian were working in a warehouse near the Pensacola Airport when it happened. Doing his job, as always, Dez walked a bag of trash outside the warehouse just as a reckless driver sped by out of control. It was a tragedy of the saddest measure. A tragedy his mother, his father, his eleven-year-old brother, and those closest to him will never forget. The attending police officer later told his devastated mother that her beloved son died immediately on impact. He did not suffer.

My friend Pat had set up an anonymous fund at a local bank for people to make contributions on behalf of Dez's family. She asked me if I would join her in handing over the check to Dez's grieving mother. After a brief hello, his mother said, "I don't know what to say, but thank you." She spoke of her beloved son with humility and grace. "Dez never told me how many friends he had and how many people loved him." She added, "It makes grieving a little easier knowing what an example he was to others and how he died giving back." As we finished up our conversation his mother added, "While I understand terrible things happen, I think everything in life had meaning at some time . . . good things happen even in times of heartache. You know, Dez was one of the few young men who had the qualities any parent would want for their children." We agreed.

Dez's memory now encourages those of us who knew and loved him to follow his high standard: to smile while spreading goodwill, regardless of our circumstances. In an instant, the shining example of a dedicated young person, with a heart overflowing with love, lost his life doing God's work; doing exactly what he treasured most... helping those in need.

> ### A life lesson in... the power of a smile
>
> Dez will forever hold a special place in my heart. His infectious smile and his commitment to honor others in spite of his circumstances was contagious to all who knew him. We might ask why would one so young with so much life ahead of him be taken in the blink of an eye? I struggled with this question until I spoke with his mother. Her words of thanksgiving for a son who exemplified the very desire God has for all of His children... to be dedicated to Him and to be examples of His great love for the time we have been given here on earth, warmed my heart. A friend once told me, it's not how many we love, but how many love us. And for Dez, he was loved and respected by so many.
>
> *Dear Lord, like Dez, make us instruments of Your peace and Your love. Let us smile as if it were our last--let us be examples of Your love, as a legacy for those we hold dear.*
>
> *Amen*

"The best thing to hold onto in life is each other."
—Audrey Hepburn

"Do all things without grumbling or disputing; that you may prove yourselves to be blameless and innocent, children of God above reproach in this crooked and perverse generation, among whom you appear as lights in the world... so that in the day of Christ I may have cause to glory because I did not run in vain nor toil in vain."
—Philippians 2:14–16

28

Summer and Shawn

"Rejoice in hope, be patient in tribulation, be constant in prayer."
Romans 12:12

When my children were still young, my former husband and I moved to a resort community about thirty-five minutes from town. My sister Kathy, her husband and their four kids lived close by, which was one of the reasons we decided to make the move. Together we had seven children under the age of twelve. One sunny afternoon I promised the children a trip to the local Gate food mart after homework and swimming. My sister stayed behind with two of our boys while I took the rest of the gang for a frozen Icee. The kids couldn't get out of the car fast enough. "I want a cherry one." "Me too." "Me three," they squealed.

As we went to the check-out counter, a friendly young woman asked, "Can I help you with anything else? I'm Summer, if you ever need something." I thanked her and we headed to the car.

In the 1990s this was the only nearby gas station. After the local grocery closed for the night, there were no other options for a pick-up snack or any last-minute items. So we ended up spending a lot of time at the local Gate station, where we saw Summer several times a week. This hardworking, dedicated young woman always had a smile on her face, but I could see that she felt intense back pain due to a weight problem and a day full of bending at work. I learned her mother also worked at the same Gate station and that Summer had a five-year-old adopted son named Shawn, with attention deficit disorder.

One day I couldn't help but notice Summer's anguish. Usually, she was so helpful and cheerful. I wanted to make a gesture to reach out to her. "Are you going to be all right?" I asked. "Oh, I'm fine," she responded. "I just have a bad back and am waiting to have a gastric by-pass so I can lose some of this weight. I've tried everything." She wiped a tear away from her eye. "The doctors keep putting me off because I haven't lost enough weight initially and I just gain it back when I do lose it. I worry about my son because I know he doesn't like me looking this way or seeing me in so much pain. I feel bad for him."

The tenderness in her voice when she referred to her son imparted a like tenderness in my heart for the two of them. I wanted to do more, but what and how?

"Can I give you my phone number so you can let me know how things are going?" I asked.

"Here is my cell number too," she said, tearing off a small piece of cash register tape, jotting down a number, and we exchanged information.

"Really, please call me," I said. "And let me know how you are feeling and if I can do anything to help."

She smiled and remarked, "Oh, thank you Miss Mary, God bless you."

Once again, the tenderness in her trembling voice humbled me. I wondered how Summer and so many others like her were going to make it. Despite the daily meltdowns with Shawn, the possibility of layoffs at work, trying to find safe and affordable housing, driving a car that spent more time in the mechanic's shop than on the highway, and several health issues related to her weight, Summer persevered with hope and courage.

That December, my older children came to me after visiting the Gate station, one day. "Mom," my oldest asked, "can we please help Summer and Shawn this Christmas? We want them to have the best Christmas ever and we have enough." I couldn't believe it. Christmas was just around the corner and my children said they had decided to go without their usual gifts to ensure Summer and Shawn could experience the joy and blessings of Christmas. They talked less and less about their own gifts and more about what Summer and Shawn might want. It was a blessing for me to see their desire to help this family in need. One afternoon, a couple of days before Christmas, I called Summer and asked if they could come by my house. We wanted to surprise them. "Oh thank you so much," Summer said. "That would be so nice. Shawn would love that."

They walked in the front door, and Shawn's eyes gazed at his presents under the tree. Each of my three children handed him gifts. He looked shocked and amazed. "These are for me?" he asked.

"Yes, Shawn," I said. They're all for you, from all of us." To see the look of appreciation on his face as he opened a large box that held the Xbox video game, which he had asked his mom for, was the greatest gift for us.

"Oh, my goodness I can't believe it," he exclaimed. "And how did you know I wanted these games to go with it?"

Summer stood back with tears welling in her eyes as Shawn tore open a box holding a football jersey and several smaller items. Next, Summer opened her gift basket filled with lotion, scented soap, a honey baked ham coupon and a gift card attached for any extras they might need during the holidays.

"Thank you everyone for giving us a blessed Christmas," she said. "I don't know what to say." The truth was she didn't need to say anything.

The look on both of their faces warmed the hearts of my children and me. It reminded me of what a friend had once told me, "When you see a person's eyes light up after sharing a good deed, it's like watching a happy child blowing bubbles toward heaven."

As the years passed since that first Christmas with Summer and Shawn, we've kept up with one another. When I was diagnosed with ulcerative colitis, Summer called just about every day to check on me or to send a text even when her minutes were running low on her phone.

Then just before his fourteenth birthday, Shawn came to stay with my family for several days while his mother had a complicated hysterectomy. Since my youngest was away at college, it thrilled me to have a youngster in the house. Shawn's energy and desire to question everything, from football to health issues and everything in between, was refreshing, but at times it was overwhelming. He asked more questions in five minutes than my son asked in a week—or maybe even a month!

"When is your son coming home from college?"

"How come he is so quiet?"

"Where are your girls?"

"Are they going to get married?"

"What are we eating for dinner?"

"Can we go canoeing after dinner and then play soccer?"

After four days and three nights I was exhausted and exhilarated at the same time. The truth is I hated to see him leave. When I told him his mother had called and was expecting him home, he asked if he could stay just a little while longer. "Oh, Shawn" I said, "You know your mom has missed you and we'll do this again soon."

Shawn nodded his blonde, freshly cut head of hair. "Okay, Miss Mary," he said. "I know my mom needs me." Slowly, he kicked a pine cone down the sidewalk as we walked to the car.

"Shawn, are there any last requests before we arrive at your apartment?" He thought for a minute. "Well," he said, "could we maybe go get my mom a card and a little something to make her feel better?"

Stopping at a nearby grocery, Shawn picked out a card while I looked for some flowers. I asked the floral clerk about one arrangement in particular. "This one is a little pricey," she remarked. "Is it for anyone in particular?"

Just then, Shawn walked up and the clerk took one look at him and . . . hugged him like a mama bear.

She looked back at me, "Oh, I'm sorry, you are?" she inquired looking at me.

"My name is Mary Ann. I'm a friend of Shawn's mother. She just had surgery."

"My name is Pam," she said. "I knew Shawn when he was just a little boy, she explained. She continued, "I lost my job several years ago and Summer's mother worked for the same company and asked me to come live with her until I could get my feet on the ground. Please say hello for me and tell her that I'm getting back on my feet again and doing okay."

These Appointed Moments, I thought, where people "coincidentally" meet can be truly eye-opening! My heart fluttered. The circle of life, with people touching and helping each other, perched itself right in my little corner of the world it seemed. Certainly I had experienced more than my share of Appointed Moments for the day, or so I thought. Shawn helped me carry the get-well flowers to the car and looked at me with the sweetest smile, and softly said, "Thank you again, Miss Mary. I love you."

I gave him a hug. We buckled up and as we drove off Shawn began asking more questions. I could hardly keep up. He took a deep breath and suddenly asked. "Miss Mary, did you know I was adopted?"

I nodded affirmatively. "My real mom had to go to jail," he continued, "and she was my mom's cousin, so my mom decided to adopt me 'cause we were already like family."

Dear God, please don't let me lose it in front of this precious young man. I bit my lip and listened. "I don't really know who my father is," he explained. "But I have a mentor who has one daughter and he sees me on Thursdays. Even though he's very busy, he took me to a football game. It was lots of fun."

Our forty-minute drive ended up being extremely informative. Shawn spoke of Summer with a sense of gratitude in his voice. "I'm glad she adopted me even though she has to work very hard and sometimes we don't know where we are going to live. Now we have a new place all to ourselves for the first time and maybe I'm going to have my own room."

Finally, we arrived at the apartment building where Summer and her mother lived. Shawn ran to the front door to greet his mother. "Mom, Mom. I'm back," he shouted.

"Hey Shawn, it's about time I got you back," she said holding out her arms just like a mama bear waiting for her cub to return. It reminded me of God's loving arms cradling us through life's ups and downs.

Summer's tenderness in times of anguish, her courage in times of fear and, most of all, her constant hope in times of despair—with her choice to help those around her—makes her such an inspiration for me and a candle of hope to others.

A life lesson in... embracing hope

Difficulties and trials are a part of life—there is just no way around it. We can run, we can deny, we can feel sorry for ourselves, we all do this at some point in our lives, but there is a reason for this onslaught of pain and frustration. God knows our frame, He knows our desires and our hurts and He also knows how much we can carry. Some more than others tend to bear the heaviest of loads. Take heart in this mysterious set of circumstances. Jesus trusts you and He knows how much pain you are in. He too has been there. He is watching to see how we adjust to the torments and trials of life. He is standing ready to bless us if we trust in Him and thank Him even through the pain. I've seen Summer and Shawn's frustration in the midst of the storm and I continue to see their smiles, their joy, and their hope, despite the constant battles they face.

Lord thank You for the example of those who persevere through the trails of life in their seemingly endless set of upheavals. Let us remember to thank You in the midst of these trials because You too, know them so well. Thank You for the positive role models You have placed around us. Remind us to seek joy and peace and lean on You—for there is no other way.

Amen

"As for me I will always have hope; I will praise You more and more."

—Psalm 71:14

"The Lord delights in those who fear him, who put their hope in his unfailing love."

—Psalm 147: 11

"And friends are friends forever if the Lord's the Lord of them
And a friend will say never, 'Cause the welcome will not end
Though it's hard to let you go, in the Father's hands we know
That a lifetime's not too long to live as friends."

—Michael W. Smith, singer

29

Celebrating Tina's Life

"We have this as a sure and steadfast anchor of the soul, a hope that enters into the inner place behind the curtain, where Jesus has gone as a forerunner on our behalf..."
Hebrews 6:19–20

Several years ago my daughters Elizabeth and Caroline asked if I would help them plan a fortieth birthday party for Tina. She was a friend of their father, who had been going who had been going through a rough time. The girls and I gathered some party items from my house and picked up a few more on the way to Tina's. I had never met her before, but my daughters spoke so highly of her and wanted to make sure she had a memorable birthday. Tina had been through an unfortunate divorce, while working and taking care of her three boys, so we wanted the night to be extra special.

We knocked on the front door. Tina answered cheerfully. Her flawless skin, gorgeous smile and beautiful dark brown hair reminded me of a beauty queen. "Thank you so much for coming," she said. "I've been looking forward to meeting you. The girls said you love decorating and I could use your ideas for the party."

We all lived at the beach, so we decided to incorporate that theme into the party. Several round tables were set up outside around the pool deck. A small bandstand area stood on the far side of the property for Tina's former husband, of all people, to play the guitar with his band! He worked as an attorney in town and also happened to be an accomplished musician. Tina's wonderful spirit allowed even her former husband to celebrate along with her.

Elizabeth and Caroline placed votive candles at the tables and put clear glass fish bowls in the center with two goldfish to be added later. We laced multicolored sparkles around each fish bowl and in between the votive candles. Tina looked thrilled.

The three of us raced home and had just enough time to head back with my fiancé for Tina's party. Laughter and music radiated through the neighborhood. We found a cozy table underneath twinkle lights that sparkled against the evening backdrop, a dusky black sky.

An hour or so later, Tina walked over and thanked us for coming. She mentioned seeing my former husband and noticed he'd left before she could say goodbye. She seemed a bit sad. "One day I hope we can all be friends," she said.

"Tina, I've found you never know what life might bring, so we just have to hold tight to our faith and pray without ceasing," I said.

She just smiled, gave me a hug and said enigmatically, "Sometimes life doesn't end up the way we thought it would be." I patted her on the back and returned the hug. She looked up with a distant smile. Words seemed unnecessary at that point. There were many times Jesus felt the same way. Silence is sometimes a comforter of its own. "Tina, have a wonderful night, it's your birthday," I said. She smiled softly.

Just about that time the band began to play "Happy Birthday," and everyone sang. By then, Tina was beaming. The party was obviously going to last longer than my eyes could stay pried open. So we said goodbye for the evening, wishing her a happy and healthy year. "Please have a wonderful night—it's your birthday," I said. "Don't worry about anything tonight. We enjoyed our time with you." This time she smiled and thanked us again for coming. Still, there seemed to be something bittersweet about the gathering and I couldn't quite put my finger on it.

Not long after Tina's birthday, she called and asked if she could stop by. Her voice quivered a bit and I wondered if she was all right. "I'll be there soon," if that's okay with you, she said, her voice still unsteady. A few minutes passed and she walked up to the front door holding a large orchid in her trembling hands.

"Tina, are you okay?" I asked.

She stood silent for a moment and I took her shaky hands in mine and asked if I could do anything to help. "I just wanted to bring this orchid and vase by to thank you for helping with my party," she said, "and to tell you I wish we had more time to get to know each other."

There was a connection between the two of us that day, as if we had known each other a lifetime. We shared similar medical problems, personal issues, and a deep desire to help other people.

The snow white orchid Tina gave me with its multiple blooms stood delicately in a hand-tiled vase with colorful sea glass encrusted in turquoise hues.

"You didn't have to do this," I told her. "It is so gorgeous. I will always think of you when I look at your sweet gift."

Tina said, "I will always remember you and your girls helping me celebrate my fortieth birthday."

Over the next several nights I found myself tossing and turning in my sleep. I admired Tina's energy and love for others, how she encouraged those around her to be better people. But she, like all of us at some point in our lives, was obviously dealing with fear and lack of self-esteem. I wanted to do something to make Tina feel better, but I realized she probably needed more help than I could give her. I decided to simply ask God to watch over her heart and soul and provide her peace. Several days passed. I left voice mails on her phone telling her we were praying for her and to please call if she needed anything.

Then one windy spring morning before dawn's light, I awoke with a jolt. For a moment I felt uneasy. A few days earlier I had placed Tina's fragile gift on my porch to get some much-needed sunlight, and as I caught my breath a sudden gust of wind riveted through my screen porch, blowing over the magnificent orchid and the delicate vase encasing it. I jumped out of bed, turned on my nearby porch light and bent down to see the effects of the fierce wind.

The gorgeous handmade sea glass vase sat on its side, still intact, except for a few jagged edges and the thick, round broken glass at the bottom. All I could think about was the precious woman who took time out of her day to bring me a gift at an inconceivably difficult time in her life.

At 10 A.M. that same morning, Elizabeth called me crying. "Mom," my daughter whimpered, "Tina took her life last night."

I was speechless, sad and in shock. I glanced out at the fallen vase Tina gave me just a short week before, and realized the fragile, lovely vase sitting there intact, its glass base now broken, was a sad and beautiful picture of this broken woman's life. The miracle of it all was that the foundation was broken, but the vase itself remained beautifully connected by the strength of the cement that held it together. Like the beautiful sea glass vase, with its fragile mosaics unscathed, Tina was painfully broken to the point of death, but left a lovely mark for all to see. Her beauty and her kindness will live on, as her spirit now rests in heaven.

The memory of her thoughtfulness and her amazing acts of kindness resonated at the church during her funeral: from inviting the pizza delivery person into her home for dinner to showering gifts on people she hardly knew. The pastor spoke of his talks with Tina about the Lord—about being born again, and how desperately she prayed for His peace and how much she longed for a new beginning. I was reminded of author Scott Peck's first three words in his best-selling book, *The Road Less Traveled*: "Life is difficult." It is at times, but in spite of the grief we all felt, it was certainly one of the most heart-warming and uplifting services I had ever attended. Somehow the pastor's words, and the surprise of a delicate butterfly which fluttered its way about the sanctuary toward the end of the service, left the friends and family at peace. Tina left a mark—a difference—that no person could ever take away.

I realized the wisdom yet again of what my faithful friend Reggie said, "Except for God's grace, any one of us might be walking down a dark, lonely road leading to nowhere." For that reason alone—regardless of our circumstances—the act of a simple kind word or deed can potentially help a person and can offer inspiration for others to do the same.

When we give out of genuine compassion with no expectations, the benefit becomes much grander. The act becomes a projection of our hearts. I am reminded when my friends ask sometimes, "Why do you do what you do?" or "Where do you find these people?" I just smile, knowing full well the Lord places these remarkable people in my life to teach me and encourage me to follow my heart and not the crowd—which isn't always easy. To some of those friends, I have asked a question in return, "What if I hadn't been there?" The answer, at least for me, is fairly simple: My family and my faith instilled a love for other people in my heart. It isn't like a water faucet that can be turned on and off at will.

The beautiful part of giving yourself to others is the incredible lifelong memories that never end. Instead of allowing a bad day to spiral out of control, take a deep breath, lift your head toward Heaven, and find someone who needs a smile, or a kind word, or a pat on the back. Broken people live in the richest and the poorest of neighborhoods. So many times they are people just like you and me. Embracing the needs of others, as Tina did, enables people to leave a legacy for their children, grandchildren and all those who knew them. By choosing to do unto others as you would have them do unto you, a flame ignites within your heart and soul that will shine throughout your life.

The most memorable days of my life are truly the days I felt overwhelmed and vulnerable, much like Tina. Days when I too thought, *I can no longer go on.* In those times of desperation—and there were plenty—God reminded me and continues to remind me of my friend. In spite of her heartbreaking choice, she was and will always be an inspiration to so many. Her beautiful smile, her willingness to serve, her love for her children, her compassion for others and yes, even her broken heart that led her to take her own life, will remind those who knew and loved her, to thank Jesus for sharing her with us. And to remember helping others also means allowing our questions and judgments, our lack of understanding, to be placed in the loving arms of Jesus—the One who saved Tina, the One who saves you and me, and the One who hung on a cross to wash away the sins of the whole world. .

A life lesson in... life 101

The beautiful multi-colored vase that Tina so unselfishly gave to me just before her passing sits in my dressing room, always with an orchid sitting inside. Although years have passed and life has moved on Tina's life and her acts of kindness and compassion will forever rest in my memory. Tina made a choice in the midst of pain and heartache that many of us cannot comprehend. But she knew the Lord. And He says He promises forgiveness and justification to those who know and love Him. His great love extends to all who know Him—He will never leave or forsake us—His promise, that holds for us a mansion filled with love... for eternity.

Dear Lord, let our light so shine before others that they might see You in us regardless of our circumstances. Give us strength in our weakness, give us hearts of forgiveness and love, and hold us in the palm of Your everlasting hand as we walk through this ever-changing journey called life. Thank You for Your many blessings in spite of our human frailties. Thank You for knowing who we are when we're not sure ourselves.

Amen

"I plan to pass through this life but once, if therefore, there be any kindness I can do to any fellow being, let me do it now, and not defer or neglect it, as I shall not pass this way again."

—William Penn, Quaker, founder of the province of Pennsylvania (1644–1718)

30

Ginger's Welcome Face

*"So encourage each other and build each other up,
just as you are already doing."*
1 Thessalonians 5:11

Not long ago I was meeting my daughter Caroline at a small boutique shoe store in a shopping plaza with very limited parking spaces. At times, we all know parking lots tend to be a formula for frustration. Who can get to the parking space first? Why did that person back out without looking? How much will it cost to replace my bumper?

On this day, instead of driving around and around, trying to find a spot right in front, I decided to park at the far end of the plaza and walk. Brilliant, right? Actually, I probably ended up saving several minutes with no frustration!

When I arrived at the shoe shop, my daughter was nowhere in sight, but I heard someone call my name. "Mary Ann! How are you? I haven't seen you in years."

It was Ginger, a friend from my hometown of Tampa who was just passing through on her way back to Tallahassee. As middle-schoolers, we were best buddies, and we were bridesmaids in one another's weddings. Even though we hadn't seen each other in fifteen years, it was as if we were meant to reconnect on that day.

For the next hour and a half, we caught up right there in the shoe store; two women exchanging words of honesty and cheerfulness with shoppers scurrying about. We could have easily let the opportunity pass with superficial "hellos and good to see you" stuff. Instead, we went with the moment.

Sitting on a pair of comfy chair cushions we quickly settled in, discovering we shared particular circumstances that brought us to our "new and improved" life. Both of us had gone through long, heart-breaking divorces. Our former husbands were dominating and influential individuals with extremely busy work schedules. We discovered our passion for creating unique gift items; I enjoyed painting small wooden boxes with shell designs, and my friend showed me pictures of her finely crafted shell chandeliers. In a sense, it felt like an Appointed Moment where we were dancing through our past, while shoppers looked on in amazement. God had given us this special time to reconnect and we enjoyed every moment. It was as if we were once again enjoying a sleepover as we did so long ago.

As my daughter checked in, we shared how close we were to our children and that we'd both been recently blessed with men who adored us and our family too. Most wonderfully, it turned out that she also had a heart for helping others. She had been a school teacher for many years sharing her sweet heart and wisdom with youngsters who soaked up her contagious personality.

Neither one of us had changed too much over the years, only our circumstances. Some of the situations we dealt with had been extremely painful and even humiliating, but through our pain we were stronger and more aware of life's true meaning. Making a commitment to help others and to pray without ceasing had enabled us to move forward.

"Goodbye Ginger," I said, as happy tears welled up in our eyes. Somehow we both saw this as a God-given Appointed Moment. How else could two women who hadn't seen each other in almost fifteen years and lived three hours apart just happen to meet in a small, upscale shoe store?

The story doesn't stop there. Quite ironically, with my recent memory difficulties, I'd forgotten about my surprising visit with my friend at the shoe store. I didn't have a recent phone number or address. So on my way to my hometown of Tampa one Friday afternoon not too long ago, I prayed that God would somehow allow me to get back in touch with Ginger. I was headed to the wedding of my best friend's daughter. With the impending excitement of the wedding I was looking forward to seeing old friends. I didn't know who might be invited because the wedding was going to be a small, intimate affair, but I was hoping someone had kept up with Ginger and might have a phone number for her.

After settling into my hotel room, I had about an hour to get ready for a post rehearsal dinner party. I rode to the event with my mother and my fiancé. We settled in at a small round table overlooking a park-like setting in the downtown area.

Out of the corner of my eye I thought I saw a familiar face. A face I hadn't seen or didn't remember seeing in over fifteen years. "Mary Ann, is that you?" a voice sweetly asked. I glanced up toward the sparkling stars and thought, *Lord, your sense of humor and timing is absolutely miraculous.* Of course it was. This moment had been planned for me, once again, by The Giver of Appointed Moments.

"Ginger, I can't believe it's you," I explained. "I'd prayed for a way to get in touch with you—I just never expected it to be so soon!"

We hugged and cried and talked until it was time to leave. She hadn't changed one bit. Her sweet spirit and her lovely manner were endearing. We talked about life's ever-changing moments and how God always has a plan and usually it's not ours. I realize there's a reason for that. He knows us far better than we'll ever know ourselves. He created us in His image and He is training us for His purposes, not our own.

I thanked the Lord for His mercy, His grace and His unfailing faithfulness. He knew how important it was for me to reconnect with Ginger. I stood in awe of His answer to my prayer and I realized that sharing intimate moments with friends is much like sharing intimate moments with our Heavenly Father.

In that unexpected encounter, the Lord reminded me that taking time to share a portion of an otherwise hectic day is simply a moment of God's grace, waiting like an angel of mercy to bestow its bounty on an unsuspecting recipient.

Our joy in life is inexorably determined by the degree to which we love."
—Seth Adam Smith, author

"The willingness to share does not make one charitable, it makes one free."
—Robert Hale, author

"The most beautiful discovery true friends make is that they can grow separately without growing apart."
—Elizabeth Foley, poet

A life lesson in... unexpected encounters

Seeing my friend Ginger so unexpectedly was like receiving a surprising gift, a gift spontaneously given. As we sat and talked I realized I had forgotten we had so much in common because the years had flown by so quickly. The events that had taken place since our last visit, almost fifteen years before, were unimaginable in many ways and yet our love of creating things and our love for Jesus and for other people kept us going. The Lord knew we would meet that memorable day in the shoe boutique, as the world around us stood still. We were able to connect and share with a crowd of onlookers who probably thought, are these two ever going to leave? God's had planned the unexpected encounter as a way for us to reconnect and catch up on old times and new. We were thankful He brought us back together in such a unique way.

Dear Lord, thank You for our friends. Thank You for those unexpected detours that fill our souls with joy and pure delight. You are an awesome God. Teach us to wait on You, because when we do, the most ordinary day can become extraordinary.

Amen

31

An Unlikely Group of Trojans

"And do not forget to do good and to share with others, for with such sacrifices God is pleased."
Hebrews 13:16

In February 2011, my son Martin and I set off on our final college-search trip. He was fortunate to have been accepted by every school where he had applied. "It needs to have Division I football and a good sports administration program," he explained. "And there's one more thing—nearby barbecue restaurants." He knew what he liked and concentrated his efforts on those particular things.

Martin told me we wouldn't need to use the car's GPS on our 2,000-mile trip; he had everything under control. My son thrives on lists and maps; everything was planned in advance so I could drive and he could direct me, including stops at popular barbecue restaurants such as Jim and Nick's with multiple locations throughout our journey. (We ate there at least seven times during the week!)

Martin is not known for being a conversationalist, so I was well aware I would be taking most of the directions through his hand movements, with an occasional, "Mom you're not keeping up with traffic," or "Are you hungry yet?"

A fishtail hand movement to the right meant get off the exit now. Left fishtail meant get over in the left lane; you're going too slowly, Mom. Pointer finger straight ahead meant upcoming exit in a couple of miles, time for lunch or a pit stop. For most parents this subtle sign language might have been frustrating, but this was his normal routine and made an effective statement.

As we traveled, Martin would scout out Jim and Nick's for lunch and sometimes dinner too. Soon I knew the menu by heart, and my predictable son ordered a barbecue sandwich, fries and a glass of water. We talked about the upcoming college football season (the prior season, just barely over), the upcoming PGA golf tournament and the next college interview.

Martin, a man of very few words, spoke the truth, the facts and nothing more, accompanied by an occasional sheepish smile. He reminded me that I always tipped too much and that I didn't have to make friends with all the employees in the restaurant! The Quiet Man and his mother were on the road again.

After one week behind the wheel, rural Troy, Alabama, would be our last stop before heading back to Florida. Driving into the small, nondescript town I wondered if my son would really want to attend college in Small Town USA. He thought his mind was already made up. Troy University happened to be number four on his list, even though their championship football team generally won the conference.

"Turn here, Mom," said Martin as we approached the turnoff. "We're finally here." "Okay, Coach," I replied.

We checked into the Courtyard Marriott, unpacked and I headed downstairs to get a cup of tea. As I walked down the hallway, a friendly housekeeper greeted me pleasantly. "You need anything ma'am?"

"We're fine thanks," I said. "Have a great night." The woman, Joyce Williams, touched my shoulder and said, "Bless you darlin." I knew she meant it by the look of kindness in her eyes. No question, we were right in the middle of the true South, and it was like stepping back in time.

In the lobby a couple stood out, dressed not in Troy University's cardinal color scheme but differently, in orange and blue. The woman held a Florida Gator pocketbook in her right arm.

"Oh, it is so good to see we are getting closer to home," I said passing by. "I'm a Gator fan, too."

The couple introduced themselves and told me they were visiting their son. The wife began, "We have met before. I met you at a political function, and I will never forget because you seemed to be so comfortable with the people who were working there, and not so concerned with the dignitaries at the event itself." I wasn't sure whether to take her statement as a compliment or not.

"Oh, it's so nice to see you again," I replied. "I do remember you lived on a street near our house."

"Yes, that's right," she said, "We're the Barnett's." I told her my son had an appointment the next morning in the admissions office. *Just another Appointed Moment,* I thought, *sent by the Lord's, loving hand.*

"You have to go see our friend Buddy Starling in admissions, if your son has any doubts," the wife exclaimed. "He was so helpful when our son was trying to decide on colleges."

After thanking them, I strolled over to the lobby's bar to order tea. The server, a soft spoken young man named Mason said, "At check-in I noticed you were with your son. Is he by any chance planning to go to college here?"

"He's still not quite sure," I said.

Mason and I started talking about the pros and cons of small schools and larger universities. He told me he'd seen how quiet and shy my son seemed to be. "I know this is a big decision and you want to make sure it's the right one." Mason continued, "I had a roommate in college who reminds me a lot of your son. He was so focused on his school work and his music, but other than that he had very little interaction with his peers."

"Actually," he said, "my roommate had a condition called Asperger's. He had a tough time interacting socially with others."

I fought back tears as this astute young man's insight hit home. "Martin was diagnosed with Asperger's when he was about sixteen. He is making great strides with the help of a physician back home." Just another not-so-chance meeting, I thought happily.

The next morning, we showed up early in admissions. I explained about meeting the Barnett's the night before and their recommendation for us to meet the director of admissions if he could spare the time. "Excuse me ma'am," said a man's voice right behind me. It was Buddy Starling. "I think I overheard my name being mentioned. What brings you here today?"

This was another one of those inspired connections I had been graciously granted throughout my life. I had to be honest in my reply: "This entire trip has truly been a gift from God. Every school we have visited has gone out of their way to make Martin feel comfortable with his transition to college life." Painfully shy in nature, Martin sat still and folded his hands. Buddy noticed Martin did not converse much. He tried to ask questions that might elicit an answer.

"Martin, what brought you to Troy?"

"I like football and Troy has a good record."

Buddy smiled, "What else?"

Martin practically whispered. "Well, I wanted to know about barbecue restaurants. I study a lot, but I like football and barbecue." I thought Buddy was going to fall out of his chair. "Martin, I have to tell you, I can't say I have ever had a prospective student be so brutally honest, and I really appreciate that."

Soon Buddy made a few phone calls on Martin's behalf and we ended up meeting Steve Dennis, the athletic director of the Sports Administration Department. Despite my son being only 118 pounds and five-foot-six of healthy skin and bones, he wanted to be part of the football program . . . somehow.

"Helping all of our students is part of the heritage of Troy University and the state of Alabama," Steve assured us. "I have three sons and a daughter, and I would hope they too would be given the chance to follow their dreams." It didn't seem to matter that Martin wouldn't be playing on the football team; he was a university student who dreamed of being involved in sports. The Athletic Director assured us of the university's commitment to God, family, and the welfare of each student.

These simple and genuine acts made us thankful for our visit to Troy University. Another set of Appointed Moments, I thought, when things come together seemingly by coincidence and yet really not a coincidence at all.

Later that spring Martin decided Troy's small, family-like atmosphere (so unlike the mythic warlike Trojans of Greek antiquity!) would indeed be perfect for his college career.

Indeed, the warm hospitality of the entire staff of Troy University went beyond the normal day-to-day issues of student life. The extra calls and visits, the thoughtful acts, have given my son confidence and enabled him to use his voice more readily than ever before; even occasionally cheering in the stands for the Trojans. From the admissions director and the athletic director to the housekeeping manager Joyce Williams at the nearby hotel, and even Mason, the deli chef, the sense of genuine warmth and compassion had inspired my son. Not to mention the University's

Chancellor, Dr. Jack Hawkins, who spent a portion of his busy morning to share with me his commitment to his students, including personally mentoring one student in particular—a student he continues to mentor and meet with even after the young man's graduation from Troy. He insisted I keep in touch if my son had any concerns, and underscored Troy's commitment to students, faith and the community itself.

What more could a mother ask for? God had certainly paved the way for my son's success, as he matriculated to college life. (An interesting side note; my family reminded me that soon after my inspiring meeting with Chancellor Hawkins, I began writing a book of stories to encourage others. Hence, *Connecting Hearts One by One*.

Toward the end of his first year, as I walked down the hallway of the familiar Courtyard Marriott near the end of the second semester, I heard a familiar voice. "Oh thank the Lord, you're back. We've missed you here." It was Joyce Williams. "I've been prayin' for that fine son of yours and his little mama." I hugged Joyce and felt blessed for the host of gracious people surrounding my son in the town of Troy. His home away from home, I thought. . . .

Much has happened of course, since that college trip and Martin's attendance at Troy. Because of my memory loss, I still have very little recollection of Martin's time at Troy, but what I do remember are the incredible lessons my son learned while at Troy.

Eventually, he transferred to Newberry College in South Carolina. Newberry, a small, tight-knit campus with a football team, was slightly closer to home and near one of his other favorite barbeque restaurant towns, Columbia.

Martin always has a plan—and prayer is a huge part of that plan. So when he phoned me one afternoon, after two years at Newberry, and asked if I could look in the mailbox, I looked up toward heaven and asked,

"What now Lord?" "There might be something from the University of Florida inside the mailbox," he said. There was. "Please open it, Mom."

I eagerly opened the envelope, which looked very official. The first and most important words written after his name: "Congratulations, you have been accepted for the fall term at the University of Florida." My shy, socially awkward and extremely diligent son had been accepted to the same university from which his father, his grandfather, his great-grandfather and his uncle had graduated. I expected a squeal or something, knowing how difficult being accepted at UF had become, but no, not from Martin. "Okay, thanks, Mom," he said. "I gotta go study now." He was finishing up his last set of exams at Newberry.

Martin was recently home from the University of Florida for the weekend and he noticed a sound bite from the TV announcers about the Troy University football team. "Mom, look, it's Troy." I asked him if he still missed being there. "Sometimes," he said. "That's where I learned a lot about life and how important it is to help other people." I shared with him my recent visit with its former athletic director, Steve Dennis, who is now at Georgia Southern. "Yeah, he taught me to never give up on my dreams. He's a big reason I made it at Troy and why I'm making it at the University of Florida." Steve Dennis and others at Troy had shared with my son the importance of helping others and reaching out to those in need. How appropriate that a heap of Appointed Moments, a couple of unexpected detours and a caring athletic director ultimately led Martin to another place he now refers to as "home."

The act of helping another person is exactly what Jesus did every day of his life on earth. When we emulate His actions, He notices. Remember, there is no telling what the actual return might be on a small, selfless investment in another human being. Maybe, just maybe, a life will be changed . . . forever.

> ## A life lesson in... helpfulness
>
> Helping others is the very attribute that God speaks of over and over in the Bible. There is no greater gift than giving a portion of yourself to another person. Both the giver and the receiver are blessed and God sees His children doing unto others as you would have them do unto you. Unspeakable joy comes from opening your heart to someone in need or someone who could just use a pat on the back, a smile or a warm word to lift their spirits. I am grateful for these moments and the people God has placed in my life.
>
> *Dear Lord, thank You for those who reach out to others in Your name. The gift of helping others is a sign of our relationship with You. Remind us Lord to choose kindness, grace and mercy, just as YOU have taught us.*
>
> *Amen.*

"In the same way, let your light shine before others, so that they may see your good works and give glory to your Father who is in Heaven."
—Matthew 5:42

"The best portion of a man's life: his little, nameless, unremembered acts of kindness and love."
—William Wadsworth, Poet

Postscript

Angel Marks, Heartnotes, and The Vine of Simple Acts . . .

I'd like to thank you for being a part of this incredible journey—a journey that has connected the hearts of these remarkable people to mine. I hope they've done the same for you. I want to invite you to join me in *Connecting Hearts One by One.* You can start an unforgettable journey by helping others in your own personal way. By creating what I refer to as Angel Marks and Heartnotes, you'll see lives change, including your own. Joy will fill your hearts.

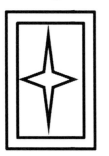

"Angel Marks" are what my children refer to as "sweet treats" from Heaven. They are unanticipated moments of God's grace, showering joy upon the giver and the receiver.

Heartnotes allow me to thank the special people in my life for being present.
I use a heart-shaped insignia to represent my appreciation of a gift, a special moment or simply to let someone know how important they are to me. I like to place them in unexpected places; on a pillow, the bathroom mirror, a car windshield—anywhere will do. You'll find your own creative nook to place a surprising and thoughtful note.

Several years ago, I was looking for a parking space in a large shopping center. I'll never forget seeing an elderly woman wandering around lost, obviously looking for her car. I rolled down my window and asked her if she could use some help. She hesitated for a moment. Then my daughter Caroline opened the back door and asked if she'd come sit beside her.

Caroline, with a heart of gold, explained to the sweet, slightly shaky woman that she had a grandmother and she wouldn't want her walking around in a big, hot parking lot by herself. I could see the woman relax after my daughter spoke to her. We found out her name was Kay, and she spelled it just like my mother! Caroline squealed after we found the woman's car. "Mom, we just gave Miss Kay an Angel Mark—she really needed one."

The Lord had actually given Caroline and me our very own Angel Mark. We met a woman who reminded me so much of my father's mother who had recently passed away. It was a blessing from the Lord, a connection from one heart to another—actually three hearts in this case, with my daughter's comforting words. I was reminded of another divinely appointed moment in my life.

One of my fondest memories was after meeting my little friend Gracie, in Chapter 25. I had dropped off a simple Heartnote at her grandmother's front door and left a beautifully sculpted wooden heart beside it. With Grace in and out of the hospital, I wanted her to have something small, yet significant, to remember our special time together—our new friendship. She, in turn, sent me a Heartnote of sorts with a whimsical drawing of her dog named Sydney. This was a day I'll always treasure. It was a connection, a gift, delivered by our loving Father to His beloved children. He is the creator of Angel Marks and Heartnotes. The Bible tells us in James 1:17, "Every good and perfect gift is from above, coming down from the Father of the Heavenly lights, who does not change like shifting shadows." What a promise—what a beautiful message from our Father who art in Heaven. Hallowed be His holy name!

Soon, you'll begin to see these Angel Marks and Heartnotes can truly make a difference in the lives of so many people. And not only do they bring joy to your heart—they're so easy. Anyone can offer an Angel Mark or a Heartnote to an unsuspecting recipient. They'll love it!

First, begin by praying for the people you know, the people closest to you, who are going through a tough time or someone who might just need a friendly "hello." Watch and listen for opportunities in your home, workplace, neighborhood, volunteer meeting, grocery store, in a doctor's office or even, as I love to do, in a parking lot! I've found God has a way of placing us together with complete strangers and simply wonderful occurrences tend to spring up.

Imparting these acts of kindness can make us feel uncomfortable, even awkward. Change can initially feel uncomfortable and challenging. For me, it took a serious illness and a hard look in the mirror to take a leap outside of my comfortable routine. Some of us tend to have an aversion to change. Remember, these Angel Marks are easy, and the prescription remains the same: There are no rules for helping others. You cannot overdose when the prescription involves only one main ingredient: LOVE. Love starts a chain reaction that allows your heart to reach out in simple and sometimes heroic ways.

Then, thinking of others I'm always inspired by Summer and Shawn, now part of my extended family and both introduced to you in Chapter 28. Their lives have been tossed and turned by the storms of life. From significant financial issues to physical infirmities, the devoted mother and son persevere through life's obstacles, never giving up hope. They live in a constant state of flux and yet their hearts are committed to one another and to the people they help. We too can make this choice—together.

The admirable actions embodied by Summer, Shawn and my other friends who you've met in these pages have helped me envision an idea for how we can reinforce our Angel Marks and Heartnotes—by creating our own Vine of Simple Acts. It begins with one vine as the starting point for an outpouring of goodwill toward humankind. Love, the strongest foundation I know, allows the vine to grow upward and outward, enlarging and reaching out to others. To use the Vine of Simple Acts, first visualize your name at the base of the vine. Remember, God has already hidden in your heart an immense bounty of untapped longing to help others! All you have to do is take the first step.

Next, choose among the attributes in the interwoven vine and consider how you might use them to help some of the people you've previously identified. For instance, you might begin with an act involving "kindness" and decide to secretly drop off a beautiful, bud-filled miniature orchid for a friend. She'll be thrilled . . . and surprised!

Now the "kindness" branch in your Vine of Simple Acts, with God seated above, has a gift of a gorgeous flower attached to it. Your vine grows over time and what's most exciting is the idea catches fire and spreads to others . . . as more and more people help out.

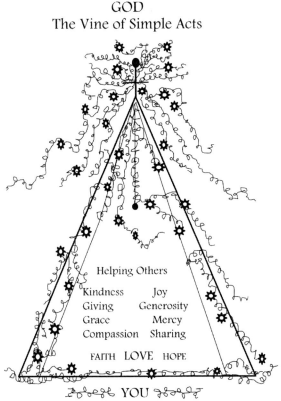

Your Vine of Simple Acts cannot fail. It can truly inspire you to make a positive change in your life and a charge to make a difference in the lives of others! A charge God encourages over and over, "Do unto others as you would have them do unto you."

Don't forget, no matter where you are in life, you have a choice to reach out or not. Whether rich or poor, regardless of race, religion, or family background, you can change the way you see yourself and have infinite possibilities to make a difference. And, like me, don't be surprised if you experience extraordinary showers of Appointed Moments of God's handiwork placed along your path. Ever so quietly, try imparting these acts anonymously. Don't tell anyone. These silent, unnoticed acts of humanity will be like a host of extra gifts to others that you will treasure for a lifetime.

One last thought: I encourage you to do an act-a-day consistently for the next month—using either your own ideas or the following 31+ 1 suggestions, or a mixture of both—so your Angels Marks accumulate and become a lifelong habit. Ask God to allow you to embrace the people you meet, the ones who might change the way you see God, yourself and others.

Now you're ready to start your own journey in helping others, filling your life with your own Vine of Simple Acts—reaching out to others, making your own difference in a world of people ... waiting for YOU!

31+1 . . . Simple Acts to Follow

- As I've enjoyed doing for years, make your own Heartnote. Write and leave it in an inconspicuous place for a person you care about. Inside a favorite book, for example, or on the bathroom mirror or under a bed pillow. It's a great way to say, "I Love You" or anything else you like!
- Phone someone you wouldn't normally talk to regularly. Tell them you are just checking in to say "hello." See what happens!
- Never forget to tell your family how much you love and appreciate them, EVERY DAY. Every time you tell them you love them . . . you are building the strongest foundation of all.
- Let two cars in front of you in traffic, instead of one. Sometimes I get carried away with this simple act and my kids do the "C'mon Mom" thing. "Enough."
- Leave a card in a neighbor's mailbox, asking, "Would you have time for a cup of tea?"
- Say hello to someone you normally would just pass by; and tell them to have a great day.
- Send a holiday greeting to someone you would not ordinarily correspond with. Any holiday is the perfect time to spread goodwill.
- If your budget permits, leave an extra tip for your server in a restaurant.

- Drop off dinner for your local firefighters. Attach a brief thank-you note (Heartnote). They love lasagna, if you're already whipping up a dish!
- Consider reading to a group of elderly people at a nearby nursing home, an assisted-living facility or an Alzheimer's day center. I'll never forget meeting my friend Annie so many years ago at The Day House for Alzheimer's. She filled my heart with such love!
- Offer to let someone go ahead of you in the grocery line. You may find a moment of serendipity.
- Find families through churches or homeless shelters that might need a helping hand and pray for them every day for a month.
- Thank a co-worker for his or her hard work.
- Go visit the children's unit at the nearest hospital. Consider cutting out a stack of hearts as you probably did in kindergarten. Share them with the kids and suggest they write a Heartnote to a special friend or family member. Even though they are sick, they love spreading cheerfulness.
- Tell a stranger, "You look nice today."
- In a rainstorm offer your umbrella to help someone to a dry place. This is so unexpected and a welcome treat for everyone!
- Give someone in your community directions if they seem to be lost.
- Go to the nearest dollar store (or even better, your own kitchen) and make a basket of treats for your neighbors during any holiday. It's an unexpected delight that makes their day. Funny thing... it can inspire others to pay it forward in their own way: like dropping off a tiny basket of cookies and jelly beans at Easter!
- Get to know the people who serve you in restaurants, gas stations, dry cleaners, cobbler shops, grocery stores, etc. It's amazing what you might find out about them.

- Take a disgruntled employee or friend to lunch. It just might change his or her attitude. Think about it.
- Help an elderly neighbor with his or her groceries.
- Offer a person working outside in your neighborhood a refreshing drink. They'll appreciate your kind gesture.
- Write a note to your child's teacher thanking them for instilling the love of learning. Tell them how much you appreciate all they do. You might inspire them to do something extraordinary!
- Pass on an uplifting book to a business associate or friend who might be going through a rough time.
- Write a Heartnote to your spouse or partner and place it on the steering wheel of his/her car, or on the outside window, (if it's not raining) or any other unexpected place . . . a great start to the day.
- Encourage neighborhood children to make the right choices and tell them "good job" when they have made a positive choice.
- Talk to the bag boy at your local grocery store while you're in the check-out line. I've met some very remarkable individuals waiting for my groceries.
- Take time to find the restaurant manager and let him or her know about the excellent service your server provided.
- Deliver cold or frozen refreshments to post office employees on an extra hot or busy day.
- Thank your local veterans and active duty military for protecting our great country.
- Remember, when you're in a parking lot someone often needs a helping hand. I have met the most interesting people this way!
- Surprise the person behind you in a drive-thru by paying their bill. This happened to me one morning at our local Starbucks and it not only made my day but was a lovely example to the young servers who

witnessed this surprising act of "paying it backward." Now, because of one person's act of kindness toward me—I love returning the favor when I have a little extra cash in my wallet. Paying it backward in any drive-thru is an extra-special surprise.

+ 1 Simple Act to Follow

- Ask the God of all hope to fill you with abundant joy as you reach out to others, making your life an example of doing unto others as He would have you do… everyday.

Before you know it, these simple acts will become a daily routine that grows into a flourishing vine. It will reach out from YOU to others, thus changing our world in so many unexpected ways. I pray you will welcome and cherish the gifts God has placed in your heart to be Ambassadors for His Kingdom. God bless you and your journey as you embrace faith, hope and love in helping others. It's now up to you.
"How wonderful it is that nobody need waste a single moment before starting to improve the world."

—Anne Frank, author

Afterword

From Whom Our Blessings Flow

Connecting Hearts One by One is more than a book about faith, hope and love. It's a book about broken up people, broken homes, broken lives and broken hearts. It's a book of stories that reveal the love of Jesus, the faith of those He has called and the hope of a future filled with His unfailing promises. The individuals highlighted in these pages might seem ordinary to some. However, their perseverance in the midst of trials, their dedication to their friends and families, and their hearts as strong as a vibrant oak tree in the midst of punishing winds, soft and beautiful as an orchid set in a delicate bud vase—make them remarkably distinct. These people are not ordinary, nor are their stories—they are honest and unique manifestations of God's awesome love. A God, whose unconditional love flows from their hearts to the hearts of everyone they meet. They have all blessed me in so many ways. Their resilient hearts and their unwavering spirit inspired me to write this book.

Looking back, I recall a time in my life when I felt the world I lived in, the world my children lived in, was spiraling out of control. For a time, my children and I felt as if we were lost in a forest with no way out. We had no map, no compass and no direction. What we did have was much more than we realized at the time: faith in our God, hope for a new beginning and love for Jesus and each other.

Five months after my divorce was final I headed to the mountains of North Carolina with my three children for a time of renewal and reflection at my parents' mountain-top hideaway. The house nestled among gigantic oak, hemlock and a variety of evergreens is a refuge for weary travelers. A goldfish pond sits in the backyard surrounded by a brilliant display of pink rhododendron bushes. A gurgling creek flows down one side of the property greeting guests and passersby. It's our family's small piece of heaven.

Driving up the steep driveway of Camp Hammer II on that brisk afternoon I heard ten of the most profound words I could ever imagine from the voice of one of my children. Out of the blue, this quiet, loving child whispered, "Mommy." I stopped the car for a moment before heading up the driveway. For some reason, I felt the need to turn around in my seat and listen, really listen. They had been through a lot and I wanted them to know I was present even if I didn't always feel that way. "Mommy, hearts can be broken but they're not impossible to fix."

"Where did you hear that?" I asked.

The wise youngster replied, "It just came into my brain." How long my child held close those poignant words before they were spoken, I do not have an answer, but they were spoken as if they'd been rehearsed over and over.

At that moment, in God's country, I bowed in awe of His majesty and the gifts I'd been given throughout my life. Even through adversity and heart-breaking sorrow, Jesus spoke through my child, to my heart. Those wise words gave me hope for our future, hope for a brighter tomorrow and a greater love for my family than I thought was ever possible. In the midst of a thorn-filled garden, a rosebud blossomed. *Life will go on,* I thought, and life did go on, just as God had planned. We've celebrated eleven years of birthdays, holidays, good and bad days, illnesses and days of absolute peace and joy since that cherished summer.

More recently, my sudden memory lapse forced me to take a break from my writing. Actually I took a bit of a break from life. I realized, once again, I had been running so fast for so long that I had forgotten to take care of my health, both physical and spiritual. God says our bodies are temples of the Holy Spirit. Somehow I had forgotten that very important fact too. I thought the harder I ran and the more my days were filled with "busyness," the more loved I would be by the Lord and others. Obviously, I was extremely misguided by my own thoughts and the idea of who my Creator was.

I found out through dealing with multiple health issues throughout my adult life that being still was sometimes necessary—actually not only necessary but essential to my recovery. Through God's word and a collection of inspiring devotionals, the Savior of my life soon began to be much more than my path to eternity. He began to show me that being still, listening to His words, and sharing with Him my most intimate thoughts, were all critical to my growth process. I had a lot of growing to do—that will never change. At least not here on earth!

God began to show me little by little that He knows what we need at the exact moment we need it. In Psalms 139:2–4, the Bible tells us the Lord knows everything about us, "You know when I sit down and when I rise; you perceive my thoughts from afar. You discern my going out and my lying down; you are familiar with all my ways." It has taken me a while to figure out the great mystery of God's supreme omnipotence. He is and always will be the same yesterday, today, and tomorrow. He doesn't change. We do, and we do it often. He is well aware of our "humanness." He created us that way. Imagine that. Our Father in Heaven knows absolutely everything about us.

The Lord deeply desires our intimacy with Him. Psalm 37:4 says, "Take delight in the Lord, and He will give you the desires of your heart." He wants us to know Him, truly know Him—to delight in Him. It has taken me a while to fully comprehend that also.

However, now that my eyes have been opened and my heart is filled with the wonder of a child because my Father in Heaven knows everything about me, I am in awe of His majesty. Even before I open my mouth, even before my mind has a chance to conceive a thought, before my eyes open to a new day, He's standing with His heralded script. He's completely calm, ever-so-wise, and watchful, knowing His child is equipped for the day. Also knowing how many times this child, ME, will forget who is actually in charge and will trip and fall again and again, and ultimately, will bow down and ask, "Dear Lord, will you forgive me this day because you know I'm so very human?"

I know He looks down and smiles because as usual He knew I would mess up and He is always right there to say, "Dear one, you are forgiven, all you have to do is ask." This is God's way of teaching broken up people that He has a plan for our lives, and that includes YOU. What seems so easy to Him, we make so difficult. He gives us the tools we need—we just need to use them. He tells us in John 15:5: "I am the vine, you are the branches. Whoever abides in me and I in him, he it is that bears much fruit, for apart from me you can do nothing."

Once we learn that quite simple piece of advice, our lives are no longer our own. We become new creatures in Him and He begins the process of renewing our lives, if we will only trust that He is in complete control, not us. Of course this takes practice. I practice and practice and I still have to admit, "Lord, once again I'm trying to steer the wheel—please take it back from me."

Not too long ago I was visiting my son at the University of Florida. Martin enjoys taking back roads and is familiar with the city of Gainesville—he's been attending football games there since he was five-years-old. We took several near miss turns and landed on 5th Street, an unexpected detour. I'd never driven down the street and didn't care to ever again, but the Lord had a different plan. I was in a hurry to get back to my home about an hour and a half away. Not until we slowed down at the J.J. Finley Elementary School traffic light did I realize the reason we were there. It wasn't for the non-descript landscape or to view the ordinary yellowish brick building that housed the students. No. Instead, it was for a very brief encounter with what ended up being a compelling life lesson that God obviously wanted me to witness.

As my car slowed down to less than 20 mph I noticed a young woman in an electric wheelchair. Her head dangled slightly to the left, her hands limp and lifeless, and her legs completely motionless. She most certainly was paralyzed to some degree, but there was something amazing about her awkward situation. A young dark-haired, olive-skinned boy kept up the pace with the sickly looking young woman. His tiny little hand was clenched around hers. He watched her as if his life depended on it—and it probably did. This precious child was walking his mother home from his school—smiling, I might add, for the entire two blocks we followed the captivating twosome.

I certainly wasn't used to seeing this kind of union between a mother and her child, but I later found this extraordinary event in my eyes was actually quite ordinary in that particular area. "Yes ma'am, we do have several similar situations at our school," a young woman stated. She reminded me that Gainesville, being a college town, housed the well-respected teaching hospital, Shands Medical Center, located just around the corner. It was a place where extremely ill people with low incomes were able to receive excellent medical care. People much like the boy's sickly mother. Tears of inspiration and joy welled up in my eyes. This angelic youngster looked as if he were escorting a queen. His smile and the way he watched his youthful mother reminded me of the unconditional love our Heavenly Father graces us with every day of our lives.

This beautiful act of love and mercy also reminded me of God's exhortation to His people: bear one another's burdens. God is well aware that none of us is fully capable of making it on our own. He planned it that way. He wants His children to learn to sacrifice as The Father sacrificed His own Son. Bearing one another's burdens doesn't mean doing so only when our bank accounts are overflowing, or when we feel like being empathetic, or when the day happens to feel right for helping someone else to cope, or simply having a little extra time on our hands. It's those times when we too are barely hanging on, when we're feeling lonely or down, when life is throwing us a basket of curve balls—that's when bearing another's burdens gets our Heavenly Father's attention. That's when unexpected blessings overflow.

A young boy somewhere in North Florida is most probably missing quite a few playdates because his mother needs his helping hand. That little boy feels the blessings overflow as he walks home with his mother after school. At a very young age this little boy has embraced using his heart—his servant's heart—to give love and encouragement to his mother. He probably has no idea the magnitude of his gift to his mother or the blessings he will receive throughout his life for giving such a large portion of himself to the person he needed most. The tables turned at some point in this young boy's life and he stood ready to serve.

I realized on that autumn day that my set of trials over the past few years cannot possibly compare to a small boy taking care of his paralyzed mother. On that appointed day, I needed to see the beautiful picture of love and mercy God planned for me to witness. It's a love story I'll never forget—it's a lesson in placing your own feelings and hurts aside for the good of another person.

God has a master plan for all of us. I'm living one day at a time, waiting for the Master Carpenter to show me His plan for my life. As I wait I take small steps forward asking, "Where do you want me today, Lord?" and "Who will you place along my path?" I have no doubt He will answer me—most probably with the answer I least expect. The answer that will bring Him the glory and leave me sitting at His feet. That's the place I belong every day. That's where my fear is being replaced by faith, in the One from whom all blessings flow. That's where hope inspires me to reach out to others in the midst of the storm. Finally, that's the place where love never ends and God's abundant blessings begin.

> "We always thank God for all of you and continually mention you in our prayers. We remember before our God and Father your work produced by faith, your labor prompted by love, and your endurance inspired by hope in our Lord Jesus Christ."
> —1 Thessalonians 1:3

Acknowledgments

First and foremost, I acknowledge the One who gave me the ability to write and the gift of loving other people—for that, a love at times I do not even comprehend, which makes it all the more mysterious and wonderful. For my family, my beautiful family, who lifts me up each and every day. Their constant love and encouragement in writing, in living, in loving, in stepping out in faith makes everything all the more precious to behold. To all the many others, thank you from the bottom of my heart. You've made my life and my book a haven of hope and courage for the future. Bless each of you, my dear "peeps." To me, you are the world. Thank you!

Sophia Amitrano
Kay Arthur
J.D. Bales
Margeurite Blocker
Dr. Richard Boehme
Stephen Brown
Dr. Gerard Budd
Ronnie Burak, PHD
Dr. Carl Burak
Vikki Cline
Mary Collany
Steve Dennis
Pat DePriest
Brett Duncan
Caroline Fiorentino
Elizabeth Fiorentino
Martin Fiorentino
Gigi Graham
Jan Gruetzmacher
Steve Griffis
Elinor A. Griffith
Lucero Griffith
Stu Griffith
Dr. Charles Hadley
John M. Hammer, Jr
Kay U. Hammer
Sara Ruth Hammer
Chancellor Hawkins
Madison Heath
Gloria Henao
Sue Hinson
Jay Jacobs
Gerry Kelly

Karen Long, PA-C	Mary McKay Underhill	Erica Vona
Jordan McCormick	Marc Periou	Debbie Warner
Jeri Millard	Mike Petrie	Mary W. Warner
Linda Miller Dowie	John Peyton	Randy Warner III
Jim Moore	Ryan Restavog	Angela Williams
Lu Ann Monday	Diana Smith	Art Williams
Jim Moore	Jack Smith	Joyce Williams
Lu Ann Monday	Frank Underhill	Ginger Wilson
Rosie Morrison	Jean Underhill	Reggie Wilson

About the Author

M.A. Hammer uses her unique voice, convincing dialogue, and deep connection to others to engage readers throughout her inspirational memoir. She has volunteered at her local homeless shelter, Mission House. She served on the Women's Board of Wolfson Children's Hospital in Jacksonville, Florida, the advisory board and board of directors of In the Pink (a breast cancer boutique serving women's needs during their battle with this life-altering disease), as chairman of The Bolles Lower School Parent's Association, chairman of Beaches Historical Society Holiday Gala, and is a former chairman of Beaches Baptist Hospital Gala. She is a long-time member of Ponte Vedra Presbyterian Church. Her love for helping others has taken her throughout the Southeastern United States, getting to know the remarkable people that God has placed along her path. The author believes there is no greater gift than bestowing love on people—all people, regardless of race, religion, or where they came from. She believes giving unto others helps promote goodwill and brings joy to the giver and receiver.

M.A. Hammer and her three children live in Ponte Vedra Beach, Florida, with their Yorkie named Gracie.

CPSIA information can be obtained
at www.ICGtesting.com
Printed in the USA
FSOW01n1754070217
30540FS